iPrepDental

Quantitative Reasoning
Notes for the DAT

Quantitative Reasoning Notes Contents

Chapter 1: Introduction

The Quantitative Reasoning section on the DAT is **45 minutes long** and includes **40 questions** from the topics covered in this binder.

A basic four-function calculator is available on the computer screen during the exam. Note that iPrepDental's software calculator has the same functions as the actual DAT calculator.

We created this binder to introduce you to all the high-yield concepts asked on the Quantitative Reasoning section of the DAT. Thoroughly study each section in the binder, and consistently review concepts you tend to miss. On our software, there is a subject test for each topic covered in this binder.

Many students are very intermediated by the Quantitative Reasoning section on the DAT. Students, however, manage to increase their scores drastically with extended practice. **Keep practicing and learn from your mistakes.** Our software provides a good representation of the most recent topics covered in this section, in their corresponding difficulty level.

DAT TIP: Note that **the more straightforward questions may appear last**. Therefore, on the DAT, **if you see that a question takes too long to answer, mark it, and move on to the next question.** You are more likely to score higher if you finish the entire section with few marked questions than not answering all the questions because you ran out of time.

Chapter 2: Data Analysis

Data Analysis is comparably a newer topic in the Quantitative Reasoning section of the DAT. This section **tests your ability to interpret and visualize data in graphical forms.** On the DAT, Data Analysis questions can appear in more than one form. On our software, we cover all possible types of graphs, so on the test day, you will approach the data analysis questions with confidence.

The Data Analysis graphs you'll see on the DAT may **include Pie, Column, Box, Scatter, and Line charts.** It is essential to scrutinize the figures and data and assure you understand the following:

1. What the information provided in the graph represents

2. What the parameters are

3. What quantities are given

4. What units of measurement are being used

2.1 Data Analysis – Practice Questions

1. A random group of boys at a local high school was surveyed about their favorite sport. The results are shown in the table below.
   What percentage of boys surveyed favored basketball and baseball?

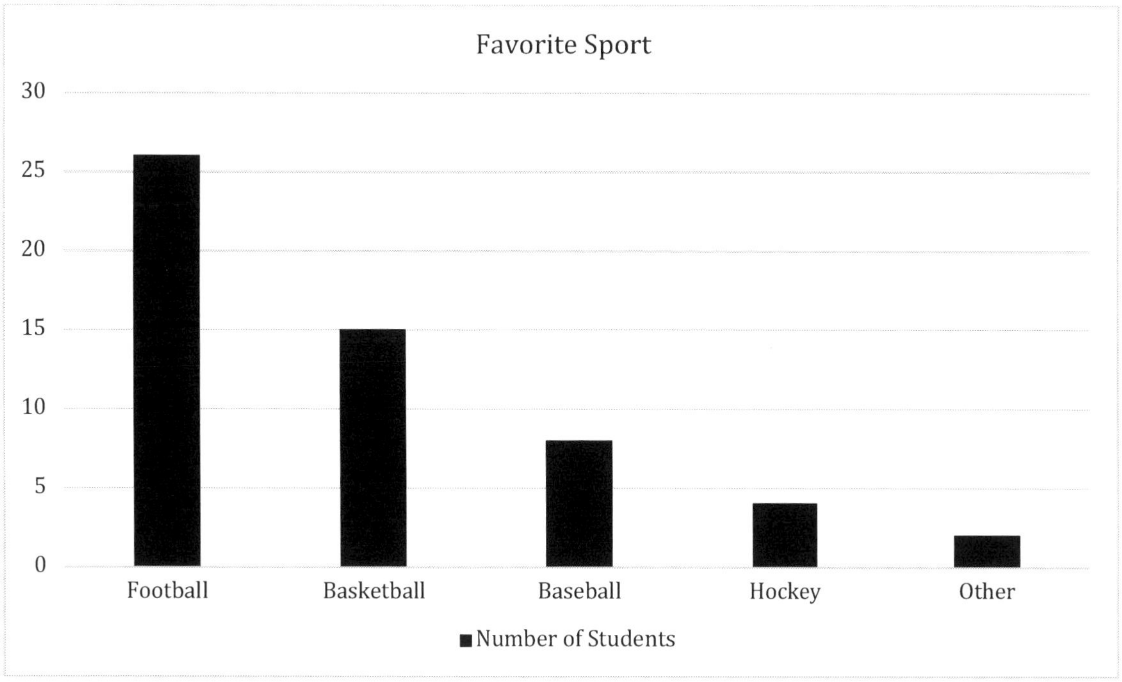
Favorite Sport
30
25
20
15
10
5
0
Football
Basketball
Baseball
Hockey
Other
Number of Students

A. 23%

B. 42%

C. 15%

D. 8%

E. 7%

2. A random group of boys at a local high school was surveyed about their favorite sport. The results are shown in the table below.

How many more boys favored football than hockey?

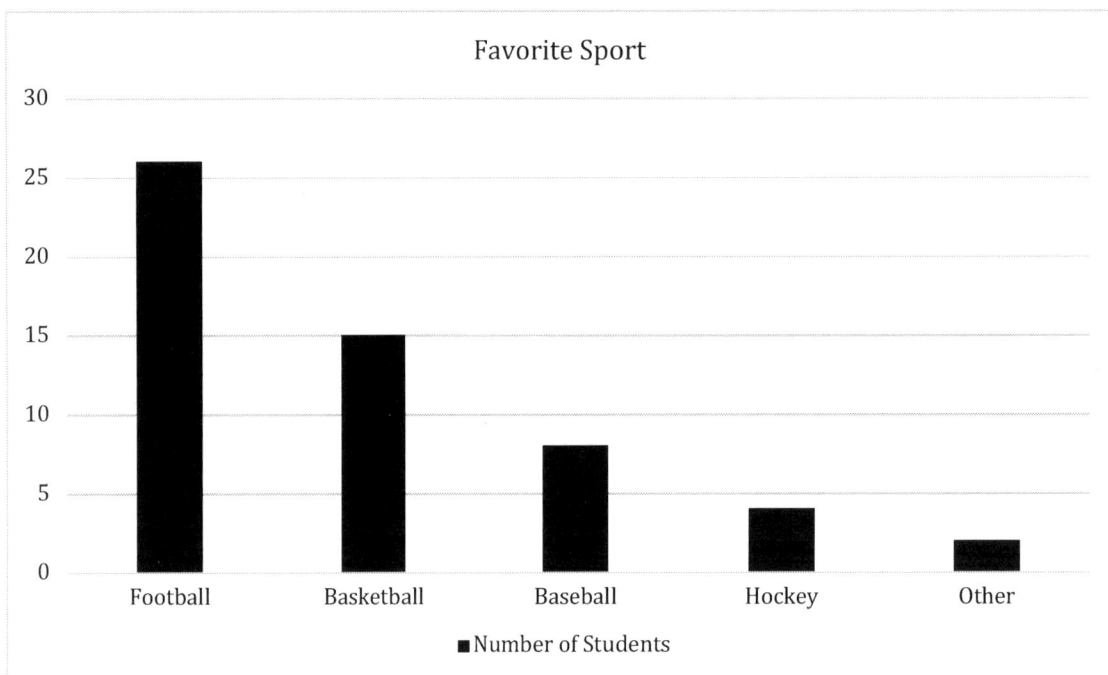

A. 26

B. 22

C. 4

D. 29

E. 15

3. A random group of boys at a local high school was surveyed about their favorite sport. The results are shown in the table below.

How many more times do boys favored basketball over hockey?

Favorite Sport

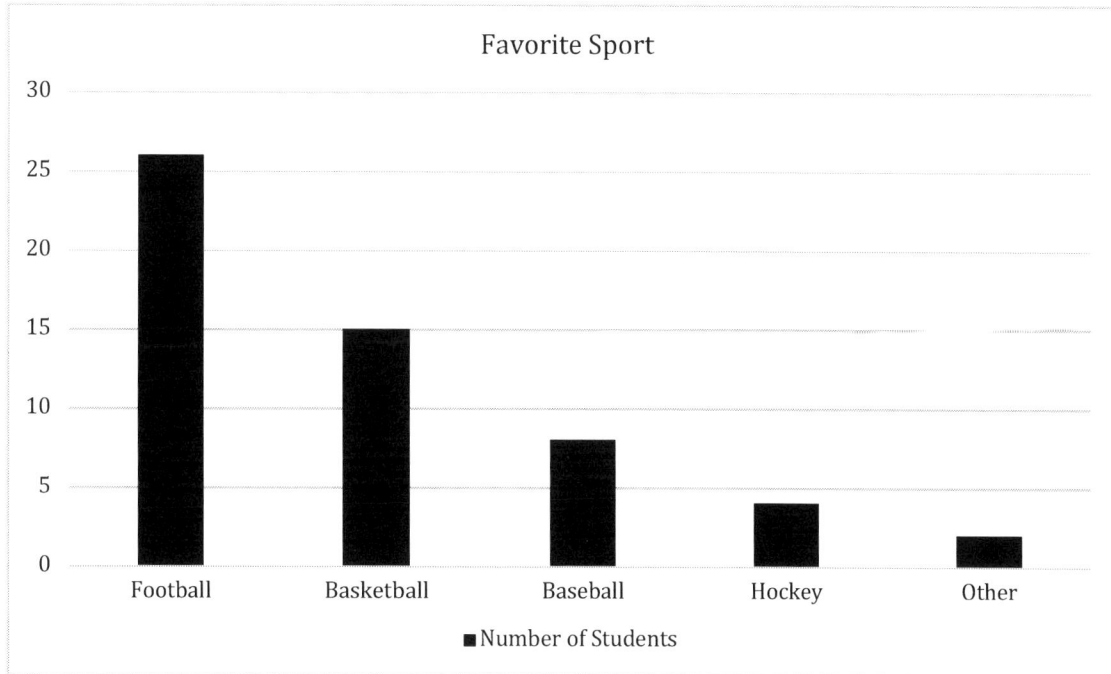

A. 15

B. 11

C. 3.75

D. 40

E. 27

4. The bar graph below shows the sales of magazines (in thousands) from five publishers during two consecutive years 2012 and 2013.

What is the ratio of the total sales of Magazine 3 for both years, to the total sales of Magazine 2 for both years?

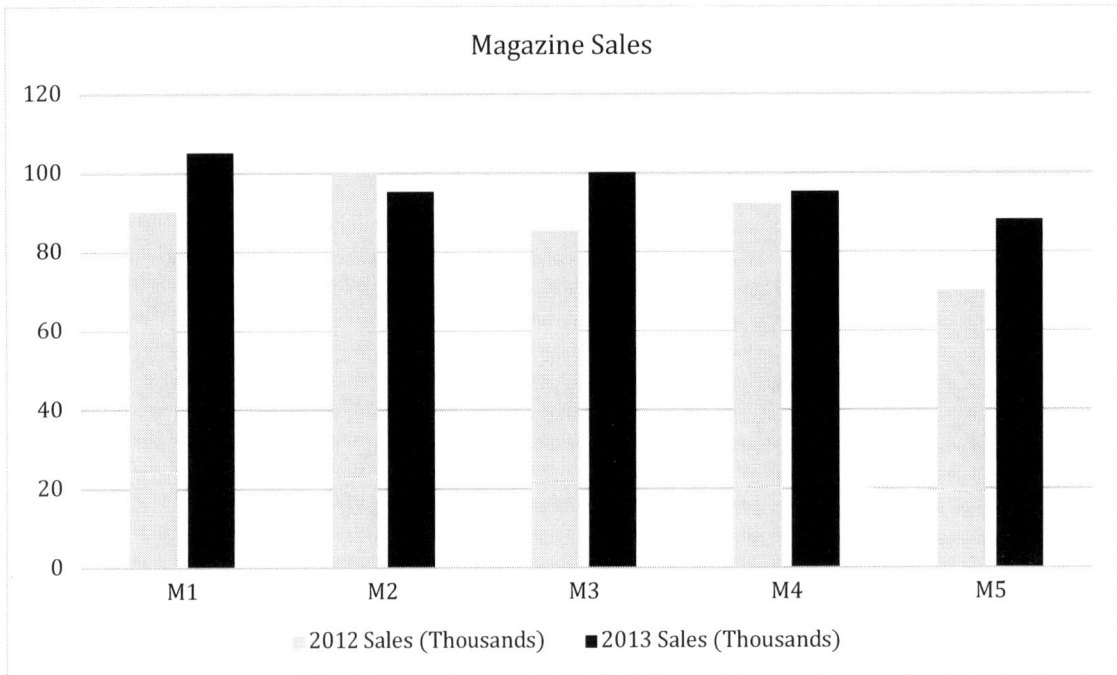

A. 39:37

B. 19:46

C. 37:39

D. 46:19

E. 27:41

5. The bar graph below shows the sales of magazines (in thousands) from five publishers during two consecutive years 2012 and 2013.

Total sales for Magazine 5 for both years is what percent of the total sales of Magazine 1 for both years?

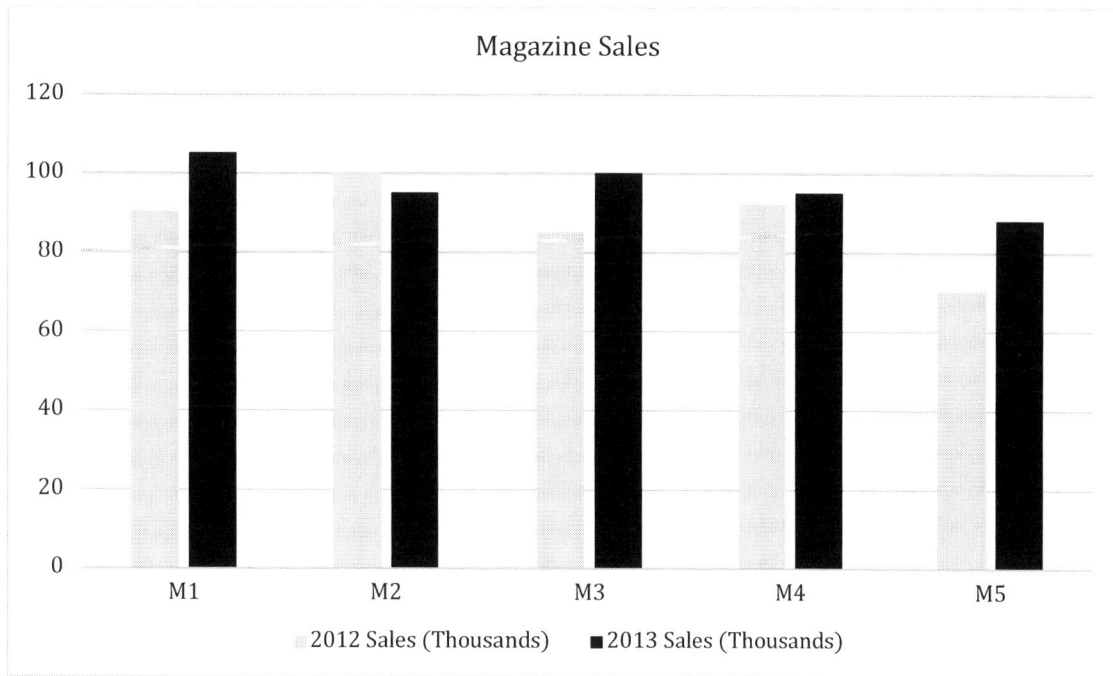

A. 81.03%

B. 92.03%

C. 18.57%

D. 76.24%

E. 84.32%

6. The bar graph below shows the sales of magazines (in thousands) from five publishers during two consecutive years 2012 and 2013.

What are the average sales of all the magazines (in thousands) in 2013?

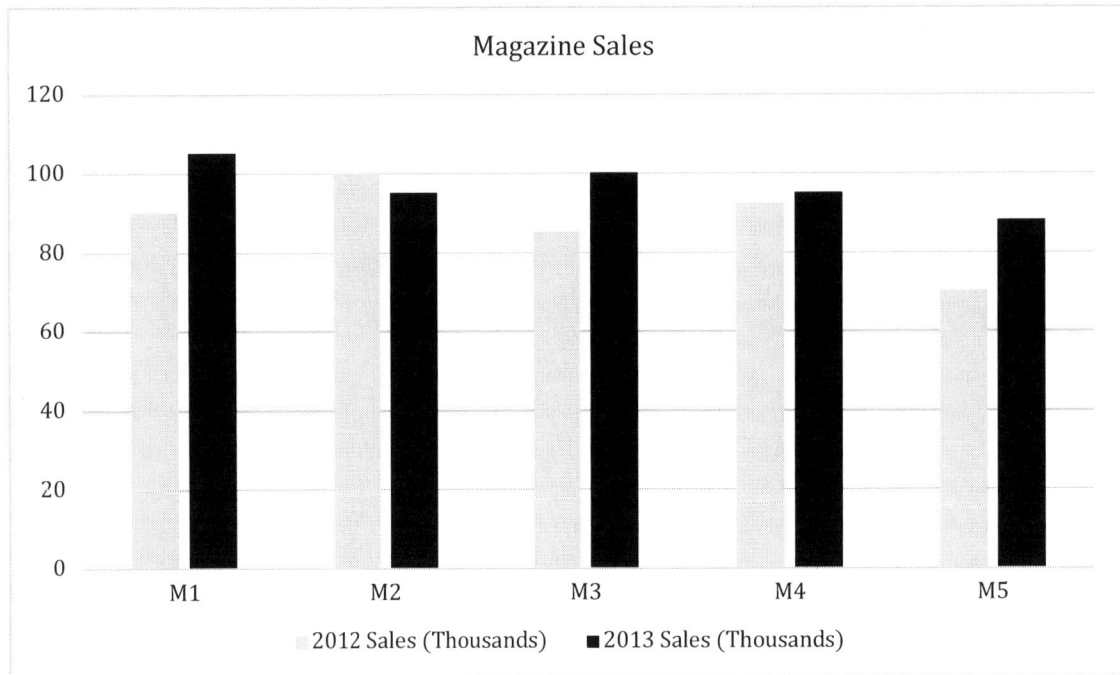

Magazine Sales

2012 Sales (Thousands)   2013 Sales (Thousands)

A. 87.9

B. 92.3

C. 85.7

D. 96.6

E. 91.4

7. The bar graph below shows the sales of magazines (in thousands) from five publishers during two consecutive years 2012 and 2013.

   The total number of magazine sales (in thousands) for Magazine 4 is approximately how many times the total sales (in thousands) of Magazine 5?

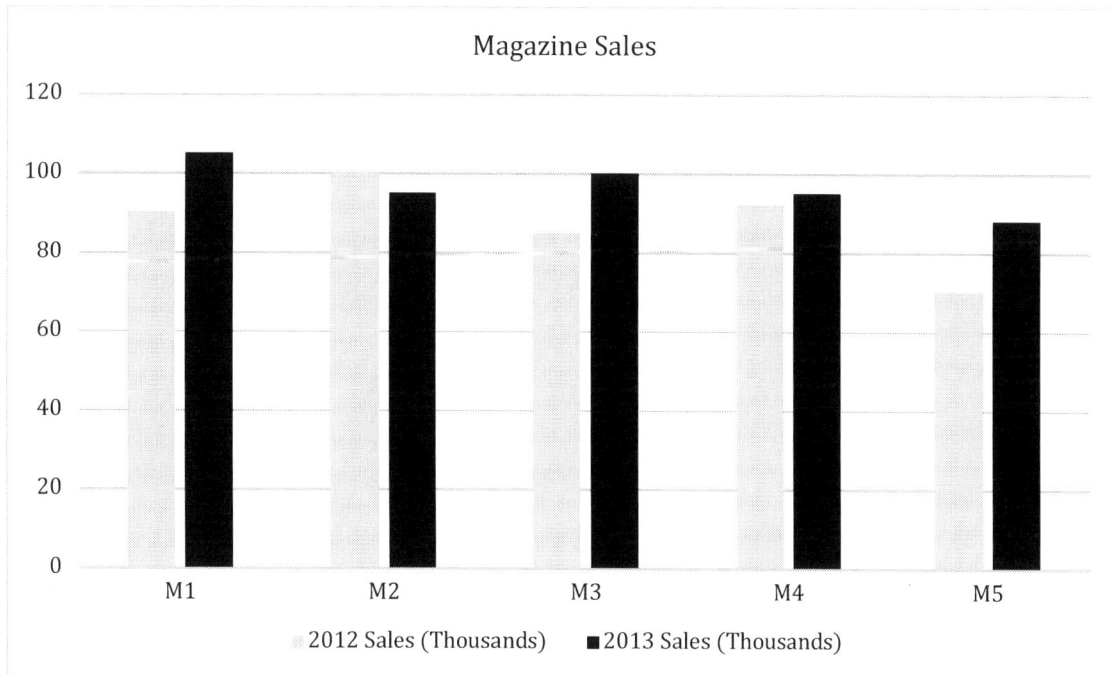

A. 2.97

B. 1.27

C. 1.84

D. 1.02

E. 1.18

2.2 Data Analysis – Solutions

1. **B.** To calculate the percentage, we need to calculate the number of favored results divided by the total number of results. Fifteen boys responded with basketball, and eight boys responded with baseball. $15+8 = 23$. If you add all the results together, you will see that 55 boys were surveyed in total. Therefore $23/55 = \sim 42\%$

2. **B.** 26 boys favor football, and 4 boys favor hockey. $26-4 = 22$

3. **C.** 15 boys favor basketball, and 4 boys favor hockey. To find out how many times do boys prefer basketball over hockey, divide $15/4 = 3.75$

4. **C.** First, find the total number of sales for both years for Magazine 3 (in thousands). $85+100= 185$. Then, find the total sales for Magazine 2 for both years (in thousands). $100+95 = 195$. Lastly, find the ratio of Magazine 3 to Magazine 2: $185:195 = 37:39$

5. **A.** First, find the total sales (in thousands) of Magazine 5: $70+88= 158$. Next, find the total sales (in thousands) of Magazine 1: $90 + 105 = 195$. Lastly, to find the percentage calculate the ratio of Magazine 5 to Magazine 1. $158/195 = 0.810256 = \sim 81.03\%$

6. **D.** To find the average, first, calculate the total sales for all magazines (in thousands) for 2013 by adding $105+95+100+95+88 = 483$. Next, take 483 and divide it by the 5 magazines to get the average: $483/5 = 96.6$

7. **E.** First, find the total number of sales for Magazine 4 (in thousands): $92+95 = 187$. Next, find the total number of sales for Magazine 5 (in thousands): $70+88 =158$. Finally, decide on the correct operation for the question. "How many times" means to divide Magazine 4 sales by Magazine 5 sales. $187/158 = \sim 1.18$

Chapter 3: Data Sufficiency

Data sufficiency is another comparably newer topic in the Quantitative Reasoning section of the DAT. It involves **a question followed by two statements. Your job is to decide if the information in the statements (taken singly or together) is sufficient or not to answer the question.**

The statement will be deliberated as **sufficient if the answer obtained is unique**. If the **question is not solved using the statement**/s **or** the **solutions obtained are multiple,** then the statement/s are considered **insufficient.**

DAT TIP: Memorize the directions and the answer choices so you will not spend unnecessary time reading the instructions on the DAT.

Directions: Each of the problems below consists of a question and two statements, labeled (1) and (2), in which certain data are given. You must decide whether the data given in the statements are sufficient to answer the question.

A. Statement (1) alone is sufficient, but Statement (2) alone is not sufficient to answer the question asked.

B. Statement (2) alone is sufficient, but statement (1) alone is not sufficient to answer the question asked.

C. Both statements (1) and (2) together are sufficient to answer the question asked, but neither statement alone is sufficient.

D. Each statement alone is sufficient to answer the question asked.

E. Statements (1) and (2) neither alone nor together are sufficient to answer the question asked, and additional data specific to the problem is needed.

DAT TIP: Don't waste your time solving the question! Data sufficiency questions aren't about giving the solution to the problem; they're about determining whether there is enough information for you to answer the question (even if the answer to the question is no). If you see that you can answer the question, stop your calculations.

3.1 Data Sufficiency – Practice Questions

1. **Steve bought a couch for $1200, then sold it a year later to Rob. How much Rob paid for the couch?**

   (1) Steve paid 5/4 of what Rob paid for the couch

   (2) Rob bought the couch for 20% less than what Steve paid

   A. Statement (1) alone is sufficient, but Statement (2) alone is not sufficient to answer the question asked.

   B. Statement (2) alone is sufficient, but statement (1) alone is not sufficient to answer the question asked.

   C. Both statements (1) and (2) together are sufficient to answer the question asked, but neither statement alone is sufficient.

   D. Each statement alone is sufficient to answer the question asked.

   E. Statements (1) and (2) neither alone nor together are sufficient to answer the question asked, and additional data specific to the problem is needed.

2. **How many girls in a class of 25 students have brown hair?**

   (1) 70% of the students have brown hair

   (2) There are 13 boys in the class

   A. Statement (1) alone is sufficient, but Statement (2) alone is not sufficient to answer the question asked.

   B. Statement (2) alone is sufficient, but statement (1) alone is not sufficient to answer the question asked.

   C. Both statements (1) and (2) together are sufficient to answer the question asked, but neither statement alone is sufficient.

   D. Each statement alone is sufficient to answer the question asked.

   E. Statements (1) and (2) neither alone nor together are sufficient to answer the question asked, and additional data specific to the problem is needed.

3. **Is the length of a side of square A less than the length of a side of equilateral triangle B?**

    (1) The ratio of the height of triangle B to the diagonal of square A is $\frac{4\sqrt{3}}{6\sqrt{2}}$

    (2) The perimeters of A and B are equal

    A. Statement (1) alone is sufficient, but Statement (2) alone is not sufficient to answer the question asked.

    B. Statement (2) alone is sufficient, but statement (1) alone is not sufficient to answer the question asked.

    C. Both statements (1) and (2) together are sufficient to answer the question asked, but neither statement alone is sufficient.

    D. Each statement alone is sufficient to answer the question asked.

    E. Statements (1) and (2) neither alone nor together are sufficient to answer the question asked, and additional data specific to the problem is needed.

4. **If c and d are both positive, what percent of d is c?**

(1) $c = 5/9$

(2) $d/c = 27$

A. Statement (1) alone is sufficient, but Statement (2) alone is not sufficient to answer the question asked.

B. Statement (2) alone is sufficient, but statement (1) alone is not sufficient to answer the question asked.

C. Both statements (1) and (2) together are sufficient to answer the question asked, but neither statement alone is sufficient.

D. Each statement alone is sufficient to answer the question asked.

E. Statements (1) and (2) neither alone nor together are sufficient to answer the question asked, and additional data specific to the problem is needed.

5. **A tire with a radius of 5 meters is turning at a constant speed. How many revolutions does it make in time t?**

   (1) The tire is moving at a speed of 2 meters per minute

   (2) $t = 30$ minutes

   A. Statement (1) alone is sufficient, but Statement (2) alone is not sufficient to answer the question asked.

   B. Statement (2) alone is sufficient, but statement (1) alone is not sufficient to answer the question asked.

   C. Both statements (1) and (2) together are sufficient to answer the question asked, but neither statement alone is sufficient.

   D. Each statement alone is sufficient to answer the question asked.

   E. Statements (1) and (2) neither alone nor together are sufficient to answer the question asked, and additional data specific to the problem is needed.

3.2 Data Sufficiency – Solutions

1. **D.** Each of these statements alone has sufficient information to determine how much Rob paid for the couch. Knowing that Steve originally bought the sofa for $1200, we can examine the two given statements:

   A. If Steve paid 5/4 of what Rob paid for the couch, let x be the amount Rob paid for the couch: 5/4x = 1200. This makes Rob's payment for the couch = $960

   B. If Rob bought the couch for 20% less than what Steve paid, then Rob paid 0.80(1200) = $960

2. **E.** Neither statement, separately nor together, has enough information to determine how many girls in a class of 25 students have brown hair. All we know from the given information is that if there are 13 boys in the class, there must be 12 girls. However, we do not know what percentage of them (or even how many) would have brown hair based on the given information that 70% of the total students in the class have brown hair.

3. **D.** Each statement on its own is sufficient to determine that the length of a side of square A is less than the length of a side of triangle B. For statement 1, we are given the ratio of the height of triangle B to the diagonal of square A. The height of an equilateral triangle is $\frac{a}{2}\sqrt{3}$ (when each side of the equilateral is a). That means that each side of the equilateral is 8 ($4\sqrt{3}=\frac{a}{2}\sqrt{3}$, $4=\frac{a}{2}$, a=8). The diagonal of a square is $a\sqrt{2}$ (when each side of the square is a). Given that the diagonal is $6\sqrt{2}$, it means that the length of each side of the square is 6. Therefore, statement 1 is sufficient to answer the question. Statement 2 states that the perimeters of A and B are equal. Given that a square has 4 congruent sides, and an equilateral triangle has 3 congruent sides, when they have equal perimeters, the lengths of the sides of the square must be less than the lengths of the triangle to achieve the same perimeters. For example, let's say the perimeter of both figures is 24. That would mean that each side of the square is 6, and each side of the triangle is 8.

4. **B.** We know that Statement (1) alone would not be sufficient to answer the question, so we need to figure out if using the two statements together, or just using statement 2 alone, or if neither will answer the question. Translating the question into algebra we get $(x/100)(d) =$ c. We know that d=27c. Then $(x/100)(27c) =$c. Dividing both sides by c, will result in x as a decimal or fraction, which can easily be converted into a percent. Notice that Statement (2) also shows this, but as the reciprocal. So, taking the reciprocal of Statement (2), then converting the fraction to a percent, would be sufficient.

5. **C.** To determine the number of revolutions in each minute, we need to calculate the tire's circumference using the formula $C = \pi d$. If the radius is 5 meters, this makes the circumference of the tire 10π, meaning the tire travels 10π meters in 1 revolution. Using statements 1 and 2 together, we know that the tire moves at a speed of 2 meters per minute for a total of 30 minutes. This means the tire will travel a total of $2(30) = 60$ meters. We can then divide 60 meters by the circle's circumference (10π) to determine how many tire revolutions were made. Therefore, we need to use both statements to answer the question.

Chapter 4: Quantitative Comparison

This section asks you to **compare two quantities**: Quantity A and Quantity B, **and then to determine which of the following statements describes the comparison**:

- Quantity **A is greater**

- Quantity **B is greater**

- The two **quantities are equal**

- The relationship **cannot be determined** from the information given

Tips for answering Quantitative Comparison questions:

1. **Be familiar with the answer choices** as they are always the same in this section

2. "The relationship cannot be determined from the information given." Never select this answer choice if each column has only one solution

3. **Avoid unnecessary calculations.** In most cases, all you need is to estimate or plug-in numbers instead of variables

4. **Geometric figures are not always drawn to scale**

5. Before you answer, **consider a range of numbers**, e.g., zero, positive and negative numbers, small and large numbers, fractions, and decimals. If one-time Quantity A is greater, and in another case, Quantity B is greater, choose answer choice D, "The relationship cannot be determined from the information given."

6. According to the ADA, this section is **not limited to geometry and trigonometry**

4.1 Quantitative Comparison – Practice Questions

Directions: In this section, you will be given two quantities - one in Column A and one in Column B. You are to determine a relationship between the two quantities and mark:

(A) if the quantity in Column A is greater than the quantity in Column B

(B) if the quantity in Column B is greater than the quantity in Column A

(C) if the quantities are equal

(D) if the comparison cannot be determined from the information given

**Information centered between both columns refers to one or both columns.

1.

Quantity A	Quantity B
$4x + 3$, if $x > 3$	$5x + 2$, if $x > 3$

A. Quantity A is greater.

B. Quantity B is greater.

C. The two quantities are equal.

D. The relationship cannot be determined from the information given.

2.

Quantity A	Quantity B
$-x + y$	$-(x - y)$

A. Quantity A is greater.

B. Quantity B is greater.

C. The two quantities are equal.

D. The relationship cannot be determined from the information given.

3. **Quantity A**   **Quantity B**

   1/a , if a is a negative fraction   -a, if a is a negative fraction

A. Quantity A is greater.

B. Quantity B is greater.

C. The two quantities are equal.

D. The relationship cannot be determined from the information given.

4. **Quantity A**   **Quantity B**

   $$(x^4y^3)^3$$ $$(x^5 + y^2)^2$$

A. Quantity A is greater.

B. Quantity B is greater.

C. The two quantities are equal.

D. The relationship cannot be determined from the information given.

5. **Quantity A**   **Quantity B**

$$\frac{3x}{8} = 9$$

$$3y = 66$$

   x   y

A. Quantity A is greater.

B. Quantity B is greater.

C. The two quantities are equal.

D. The relationship cannot be determined from the information given.

6. **Quantity A**   **Quantity B**

$$x < 3 < y$$

$x + 3$ y - 3

A. Quantity A is greater.

B. Quantity B is greater.

C. The two quantities are equal.

D. The relationship cannot be determined from the information given.

4.2 Quantitative Comparison – Solutions

1. **B**. If you plug-in numbers greater than 3 into both equations (for example, 3.1, 4, 10, 100), you will find that quantity B will always be larger.

2. **C**. For column B, using the distributive property, $- (x - y) = -x + y$, which is equal to the expression in column A.

3. **B**. Plug - in a negative fraction for a, for example, -2/3. Column A will always have a negative answer, whereas column B will always have a positive answer. Therefore, column B is always greater.

4. **D**. Let $x - 0$, and $y = 0$, then both columns equal 0. If $x = 1$, and $y = 2$, then column A is greater. Therefore, the answer cannot be determined.

5. **A**. Solving for x in Column A, $x = 24$ ($3x = 72$, $x = 24$). Solving for y in Column B, $y = 22$ ($66/3 = 22$). Therefore, Column A is greater.

6. **D**. Because $x < 3$, Column A can equal any value less than 3. Because y is greater than 3, Column B can equal any value larger than 3. Let's say $x = 2$, and $y = 4$, then Column A is greater. But let's say $x = 2$, and $y = 10$, then column B is greater. Since there is no definite answer, the relationship cannot be determined.

Chapter 5: Conversions

5.1 Temperature Conversions

- Celsius to Kelvin: $K = {}^{\circ}C + 273$

- Kelvin to Celsius: ${}^{\circ}C = K - 273$

- Fahrenheit to Celsius: ${}^{\circ}C = (F\text{-}32) \times \frac{5}{9}$

- Celsius to Fahrenheit: $F = {}^{\circ}C \left(\frac{9}{5}\right) + 32$

- Fahrenheit to Kelvin: $K = (F\text{-}32) \times \frac{5}{9} + 273$

- Kelvin to Fahrenheit: $F = (K\text{-}273) \times \frac{9}{5} + 32$

5.2 Time Conversions

- 1 minute = 60 seconds = 6000 milliseconds

- 1 hour = 60 minutes = 3600 seconds

- 1 day = 24 hours = 1440 minutes

- 1 week = 7 days = 168 hours

- 1 month = 4 weeks = 30 days

- 1 year = 12 month = 52 weeks

- 1 decade = 10 years − 120 months

- 1 century = 10 decades = 100 years

5.3 Weight Conversions

- 1 milligrams = 1000 microgram = $0.001(1 \times 10^{-3})$ grams = 0.000035 ounces

- 1 gram = 1000 milligram = 0.035 ounces = 0.001 kilogram

- 1 ounce = 28.25 grams = 0.0625 pounds = 0.028 kilograms

- 1 pound = 453.6 grams = 16 ounces = 0.45 kilograms

- 1 kilogram = 1000 grams = 35.3 ounces = 2.2 pounds

5.4 Length / Distance Conversions

- 1 cm = 10mm
- **100 cm = 1 meters**
- **1 km = 1000 meters**
- **1 inch** = 25.4 millimeters = **2.54 centimeters** = 0.08 feet
- **1 foot** = 304.8 millimeters = 30.48 centimeters = **12 inches**
- **1 mile = 5280 feet = 1.6 km**
- **1 yard** = 36 inches = **3 feet = 0.91 meters**
- 1 Furlong = 220 yards
- 1 meter = 39.37 inches = 3.28 feet = 1.09 yards
- 1 kilometer = 1093.61 yards = 1000 meters = 0.62 miles

5.5 Liquid Conversions

- 1 liter = 1000 milliliters
- 1 Kiloliter = 1,000,000 milliliters

5.6 Dimensional Analysis

Dimensional analysis is a simple way to convert between units. The goal is to use conversion factors to cancel out units, by placing them on the opposite side of the fraction:

$$\text{Given unit} \times \frac{\text{desired unit}}{\text{given unit}} \times \frac{\text{new desired unit}}{\text{desired unit}} = \text{new desired unit}$$

5.7 Conversions – Practice Questions

1. What is the Kelvin equivalent of 95 degrees Fahrenheit?

    A. 308

    B. 294

    C. 314

    D. 298

    E. 302

2. What is the approximate equivalent of 25 Kelvin in degrees Celsius?

    A. -298

    B. 298

    C. -248

    D. 248

    E. 348

3. Given that 1 inch = 2.54 centimeters, approximately how many yards are there in 8 meters?

    A. 7

    B. 8

    C. 9

    D. 10

    E. 11

4. If a bird flies at 30 miles per hour, and a bug travels at 70 feet per hour, how many times faster does the bird travel than the bug?

    A. 4,835

    B. 3,520

    C. 2,263

    D. 5,293

    E. 4,395

5. Stacey rides her bike 8 miles due south, and then 8 miles due east, on a flat road. What is the shortest distance she can ride her bike back to where she started?

    A. 19.8 km

    B. 16.7 km

    C. 17.2 km

    D. 18.1 km

    E. 17.6 km

5.8 Conversions – Solutions

1. **A.** To find the Kelvin equivalent of 95 degrees Fahrenheit, we can use the formula F =(9/5)(k – 273) + 32, and plug in 95 for F.

$$95 = \left(\frac{9}{5}\right)(k - 273) + 32$$

$$63 = \left(\frac{9}{5}\right)(k - 273)$$

$$63\left(\frac{5}{9}\right) = k - 273$$

$$35 = k - 273$$

$$35 + 273 = k$$

$$308 = k$$

2. **C.**

$$25 = C + 273$$

$$-248 = C$$

3. **C.** Dimensional analysis is a simple way to convert between units. The goal is to use conversion factors to cancel out units, by placing them on the opposite side of the fraction.

$$8 \text{ meters} \times \frac{100 \text{ cm}}{1 \text{ meter}} \times \frac{1 \text{ in}}{2.54 \text{ cm}} \times \frac{1 \text{ ft}}{12 \text{ inches}} \times \frac{1 \text{ yd}}{3 \text{ ft}} = 8.75 \text{ yards}$$

4. **C.** First, convert the bird's speed from miles per hour to feet per hour, to match the units of the bug:

$$\frac{30 \; \cancel{mi}}{1 \; hr} \times \frac{5280 \; ft}{1 \; \cancel{mi}} = \frac{158{,}400 \; ft}{hr}$$

To find how many times faster the bird is than the bug, you will need to divide:

$$\frac{158{,}400 \; ft}{70} = \text{approximately } 2{,}263$$

5. **D.** This problem combines conversions with geometry. Since Stacey rides due south and then due east, to get back to where she started, she would be creating a right triangle, where the route home would be the hypotenuse, and the 8 miles south and east would be the legs. First, calculate the distance back home in miles, using the Pythagorean Theorem:

$$a^2 + b^2 = c^2$$

$$8^2 + 8^2 = c^2$$

$$64 + 64 = c^2$$

$$128 = c^2$$

$$\sqrt{128} = c$$

$$11.3 = c$$

Next, convert 11.3 miles into km.

$$11.3 \; \cancel{miles} \times \frac{1.6 \; km}{1 \; \cancel{mile}} = 18.08 \; km$$

For the DAT, you are expected to know that there are 1.6 km in a mile.

Chapter 6: Numerical Calculations

6.1 Perfect Squares

For the DAT, memorize the list of **perfect squares** below for faster calculations:

- $1^2 = 1$
- $2^2 = 4$
- $3^2 = 9$
- $4^2 = 16$
- $5^2 = 25$
- $6^2 = 36$
- $7^2 = 49$
- $8^2 = 64$
- $9^2 = 81$
- $10^2 = 100$
- $11^2 = 121$
- $12^2 = 144$
- $13^2 = 169$
- $14^2 = 196$
- $15^2 = 225$
- $16^2 = 256$
- $17^2 = 289$
- $18^2 = 324$
- $19^2 = 361$
- $20^2 = 400$

6.2 Cube Root of a Number

To find the cube root of any number, find a number which when multiplied three times by itself gives the original number. For example, for 8, the cube root will be 2 since $2 \times 2 \times 2 = 8$.

For the DAT, it is useful to memorize the list of **cube roots** below:

- $\sqrt[3]{1} = 1$
- $\sqrt[3]{8} = 2$
- $\sqrt[3]{27} = 3$
- $\sqrt[3]{64} = 4$
- $\sqrt[3]{125} = 5$
- $\sqrt[3]{216} = 6$

6.3 Square Roots

For the DAT, memorize the list of **square roots** below for faster calculations:

- $\sqrt{0} = 0$
- $\sqrt{1} = 1$
- $\sqrt{2} = 1.41$
- $\sqrt{3} = 1.73$
- $\sqrt{4} = 2$
- $\sqrt{5} = 2.23$

- $\sqrt{6} = 2.45$
- $\sqrt{7} = 2.64$
- $\sqrt{8} = 2.82$
- $\sqrt{9} = 3$
- $\sqrt{10} = 3.16$

DAT TIP: When taking a **square root of an even exponent, divide the exponent by 2**.

Ex: $\sqrt{4 \times 10^6} = 2 \times 10^3$

6.4 Fractions and Decimals

For the DAT, memorize the list of **fractions and decimals** below for faster calculations:

- $\frac{1}{2} = 0.5 = 50\%$
- $\frac{1}{3} = 0.33 = 33\%$
- $\frac{1}{4} = 0.25 = 25\%$
- $\frac{1}{5} = 0.2 = 20\%$

- $\frac{1}{6} = 0.16 = 16\%$
- $\frac{1}{7} = 0.14 = 14\%$
- $\frac{1}{8} = 0.125 = 12.5\%$
- $\frac{1}{9} = 0.11 = 11\%$
- $\frac{1}{10} = 0.1 = 10\%$

After you memorize all the fractions from $\frac{1}{2} \to \frac{1}{10}$ calculating fractions becomes easier!!

1. $\frac{3}{5} = ?$

$$\frac{1}{5} = 0.2$$

$$\frac{3}{5} = \frac{1}{5} \times 3 = 0.2 \times 3 = 0.6$$

2. $\frac{4}{7} = ?$

$$\frac{1}{7} = 0.14$$

$$\frac{4}{7} = \frac{1}{7} \times 4 = 0.14 \times 4 = 0.56$$

Fraction Comparison

Comparing fractions to **find which fraction is larger**, is a common question on the DAT. There are two ways to answer these types of questions:

1. **Using a calculator** – my favorite method! Fast and easy.

2. **Equating the denominator or the numerator** (i.e., $\frac{5}{6}$ vs. $\frac{3}{8}$ can be written as $\frac{20}{24}$ vs. $\frac{9}{24}$)

Addition/ Subtraction/ Division/ Multiplication of Fractions

Addition: $\frac{a}{b} + \frac{c}{d} = \frac{ad+bc}{bd}$ (bd is the common denominator)

Example:

$$\frac{2}{3} + \frac{1}{4} = \frac{8+3}{12} = \frac{11}{12}$$

Subtraction: $\frac{a}{b} - \frac{c}{d} = \frac{ad - bc}{bd}$

Example:

$$\frac{2}{3} - \frac{1}{4} = \frac{8 - 3}{12} = \frac{5}{12}$$

Division:

$$\frac{a}{\left(\frac{b}{c}\right)} = \frac{ac}{b}$$

$$\frac{\left(\frac{a}{b}\right)}{c} = \frac{a}{bc}$$

Examples:

$$\frac{\frac{1}{2}}{4} = \frac{1 \times 4}{2} = \frac{4}{2} = 2$$

$$\frac{\frac{1}{3}}{2} = \frac{1}{2 \times 3} = \frac{1}{6}$$

Multiplication:

$$a\left(\frac{b}{c}\right) = \frac{ab}{c}$$

Example:

$$\frac{2}{4} \times \frac{3}{5} = \frac{6}{20} = \frac{3}{10}$$

Finding the nᵗʰ Digit of a Repeating Decimal

Example: **What is the 205ᵗʰ digit (to the right of the decimal point) of the repeating decimal 0.82498249....**

To answer this question, note that the base unit of repetition is "8249". To find the 205ᵗʰ digit, we divide 205 by four (since there are 4 digits in the base unit) and get 51.25. That means 51 complete sets of 4 numbers plus a reminder of 1 (since 0.25 = ¼). Therefore, the answer is 8, which is the 1ˢᵗ digit in this base unit.

- If after the division there is **no remainder**, the answer is the **4ᵗʰ digit of the base unit**
- If after the division there is a **remainder of 1**, the answer is the **1ˢᵗ digit of the base unit**
- If after the division there is a **remainder of 2**, the answer is the **2ⁿᵈ digit of the base unit**
- If after the division there is a **remainder of 3**, the answer is the **3ʳᵈ digit of the base unit**

6.5 Percent Word Problems

Use the table below to translate percent word problems into a math expression:

Word	Math expression
what	Variable (i.e., x, y)
is	= (equal)
of	× (times)
percent	/ 100 (divide by 100)
More than	+
Less than	-

Symbol	Words Used
+	Addition, Add, Sum, Plus, Increase, Total
-	Subtraction, Subtract, Minus, Less, Difference, Decrease, Take Away, Deduct
x	Multiplication, Multiply, Product, By, Times, Lots Of
÷	Division, Divide, Quotient, Goes Into, How Many Times

Example: **What percent of 50 is 50 percent of 30?**

$$\frac{x}{100} \times 50 = \frac{50}{100} \times 30$$

$$\frac{50x}{100} = \frac{50 \times 30}{100}$$

$$x = 30$$

DAT TIP: When solving percent word problems with an increase or decrease in price, it is helpful to **set the original price as 1**, which means 100%. Then, **any increase or decrease in price is relative to 1**. For example, if an item increases by 20%, the new price is 1.2 of the original price. On the other hand, if the price decreases by 30%, the new price is 0.7 of the original price.

Example:

A bookstore has a 15% off sale. If the price of a book is \$20, what would be its sale price?

The sale price is 0.85 of the original price:

Sale price = 20 x 0.85 = \$17

6.6 Arithmetic Mean/ Average

$$Average = \frac{a_1 + a_2 + \cdots a_n}{n}$$

Example:

If the average of x and y is 30, and the average of y and z is 50, what is the value of z-x?

$$\frac{x+y}{2} = 30 \text{, thus, } x + y = 60$$

$$\frac{y+z}{2} = 50 \text{, thus, } y + z = 100$$

$$(y + z) - (x + y) = z - x = 100 - 60 = 40$$

6.7 Scientific Notation Rules

A number in scientific notation needs to be a number greater than 1, but less than 10, multiplied by 10 to a power.

A **negative exponent** indicates the number of places that the decimal point is shifted to the left. When converting to scientific notations, place the decimal point after the first non-zero digit, and count the **number of places the decimal point has moved to the right. The negative exponent will increase by that number (would become more negative).**

Ex:

$$0.14 \times 10^{-5} = 1.4 \times 10^{-6}$$

> Notice that when we **move the decimal to the right** the exponent **becomes more negative**!

$$0.015 \times 10^{-3} = 1.5 \times 10^{-5}$$

$$0.0013 \times 10^{-4} = 1.3 \times 10^{-7}$$

A **positive exponent** indicates that the decimal point is moved that number of places to the right. When converting to scientific notations, place the decimal point after the first non-zero digit, and count the **number of places the decimal point has moved. The positive exponent will decrease by that number (would become less positive).**

Ex:

$$0.14 \times 10^{5} = 1.4 \times 10^{4}$$

$$0.015 \times 10^{3} = 1.5 \times 10^{1}$$

$$0.0013 \times 10^{4} = 1.3 \times 10^{1}$$

When **dividing two numbers expressed in scientific notation**, divide the coefficient, and subtract the exponents. Remember that - (-)= +

$$\frac{1.5 \times 10^{-4}}{3 \times 10^{-2}} = \frac{15 \times 10^{-5}}{3 \times 10^{-2}} = 5 \times 10^{-3}$$

$$\boxed{-5-(-2) = -3}$$

$$\frac{5.9 \times 10^{-3}}{3 \times 10^{-1}} = \frac{59 \times 10^{-4}}{3 \times 10^{-1}} = \frac{60 \times 10^{-4}}{3 \times 10^{-1}} \cong 20 \times 10^{-3}$$

$$\boxed{-4-(-1) = -3}$$

6.8 Rounding Numbers

When you **round up the numerator, your calculations** would always be **HIGHER than the ACTUAL** answer, so choose an answer choice that is slightly lower.

Ex:

$$\frac{0.28 \times 10^{-6}}{5 \times 10^{-4}} = \frac{28 \times 10^{-8}}{5 \times 10^{-4}} \cong \frac{30 \times 10^{-8}}{5 \times 10^{-4}} \cong 6 \; x \; 10^{-4}$$

The **actual answer** is 5.6 x 10^{-4}, which is **slightly lower** than our calculated answer.

When you **round down the numerator, your calculations** would always be **LOWER than the ACTUAL** answer, so choose an answer choice that is slightly higher.

Ex:

$$\frac{0.32 \times 10^{-6}}{5 \times 10^{-4}} = \frac{32 \times 10^{-8}}{5 \times 10^{-4}} \cong \frac{30 \times 10^{-8}}{5 \times 10^{-4}} \cong 6 \times 10^{-4}$$

The **actual answer** is 6.4 x 10^{-4}, which is **slightly higher** than our calculated answer.

When you **round up the denominator, your calculations** would always be **LOWER than the ACTUAL answer**, so choose an answer choice that is slightly higher.

Ex:

We always want the **numerator to be larger** than the denominator

$$\frac{0.30 \times 10^{-6}}{0.48 \times 10^{-4}} = \frac{300 \times 10^{-9}}{48 \times 10^{-4}} \cong \frac{300 \times 10^{-9}}{50 \times 10^{-6}} \cong 6 \times 10^{-3}$$

The **actual answer** is 6.25×10^{-3}, which is **slightly higher** than our calculated answer.

When you **round down the numerator, your calculations** would always **be LOWER than the ACTUAL answer**, so choose an answer choice that is slightly lower.

Ex:

$$\frac{0.30 \times 10^{-6}}{0.52 \times 10^{-4}} = \frac{300 \times 10^{-9}}{52 \times 10^{-6}} \cong \frac{300 \times 10^{-9}}{50 \times 10^{-6}} \cong 6 \times 10^{-3}$$

The **actual answer** is 5.77×10^{-3}, which is **slightly lower** than our calculated answer.

6.9 Approximation

$$\sqrt{128} = ?$$

Since more than likely you do not know what the square root of 128 is, we would use approximation:

$$10^2 = 100$$

$$11^2 = 121$$

$$12^2 = 144$$

So, the answer must be between 11 and 12, but closer to 11! The actual answer is 11.3!

6.10 Exponential Notation and Radicals

- $x^a \cdot x^b = x^{a+b}$ (i.e., $2^3 \times 2^4 = 2^{3+4} = 2^7$)

- $x^a \cdot y^a = (x \cdot y)^a$ (i.e., $3^2 \times 4^2 = 12^2$)

- $\frac{x^a}{x^b} = x^{a-b} = \frac{1}{a^{b-a}}$ (i.e., $\frac{2^7}{2^3} = 2^{7-3} = 2^4$)

- $\frac{x^a}{y^a} = \left(\frac{x}{y}\right)^a$ (i.e., $\frac{2^7}{3^7} = \left(\frac{2}{3}\right)^7$)

- $(x^a)^b = x^{ab}$ (i.e., $(2^3)^4 = 2^{12}$)

- $\left(\frac{x}{y}\right)^{-a} = \left(\frac{y}{x}\right)^a = \frac{y^a}{x^a}$ (i.e., $\left(\frac{4}{2}\right)^{-2} = \left(\frac{2}{4}\right)^2$)

- $x^{-a} = \frac{1}{x^a}$ (i.e., $3^{-2} = \frac{1}{3^2} = \frac{1}{9}$)

- $(xy)^a = x^a y^a$ (i.e., $(2x3)^4 = 2^4 \times 3^4$)

- $x^0 = 1, \ x \neq 0$

- $\sqrt{x} = x^{\frac{1}{2}}$ (i.e., $\sqrt{4} = 4^{\frac{1}{2}} = 2$)

- $\sqrt[a]{x} = x^{\frac{1}{a}}$ (i.e., $\sqrt[2]{x} = x^{1/2}$)

- $\sqrt[a]{x^b} = x^{\frac{b}{a}}$ (i.e., $\sqrt[4]{2^3} = 2^{\frac{3}{4}}$)

- $\sqrt[b]{\sqrt[a]{x}} = \sqrt[ab]{x}$ (i.e., $\sqrt[4]{\sqrt[3]{2}} = \sqrt[3x4]{2}$)

- $\sqrt[a]{\frac{x}{y}} = \frac{\sqrt[a]{x}}{\sqrt[a]{y}}$ (i.e., $\sqrt[3]{\frac{27}{8}} = \frac{\sqrt[3]{27}}{\sqrt[3]{8}}$)

- $0^x = 0, \ 0^0 = $ undefined

6.11 Percent Increase/ Decrease Formula

$$\text{Percent change} = \frac{[New\ value\ ]-[Old\ value]}{[Old\ value]} \times 100\% \ \text{ or } \ \frac{Difference}{Original} \times 100\%$$

- If the result is **positive**, it is an **increase**

- If the result is **negative**, it is a **decrease**

6.12 Log rules

- $\log_a(xy) = \log_a(x) + \log_a(y)$

- $\log_a\left(\frac{x}{y}\right) = \log_a x - \log_a y$

- $\log_a(x^r) = r\log_a x$

- $\log_a x = y$, $a^y = x$

- $\log_a a = 1$

- $\log_a a^x = x$

- $a^{\log_a x} = x$

- $\log x = a \ is\ the\ same\ as\ x = 10^a$

- $\log_b x = \frac{\log_a x}{\log_a b}$

Examples:

- $\log_{10}(2x3) = \log_{10} 2 + \log_{10} 3$

- $\log_{10}\left(\frac{6}{4}\right) = \log_{10} 6 - \log_{10} 4$

- $\log_{10}(2^8) = 8\log_{10} 2$

- $\log_2 x = 3, 2^3 = x = 8$

- $\log_5 5 = 1$

- $\log_2 2^4 = 4\log_2 2 = 4$

- $4^{\log_4 2} = 2$

- $\log_2 8 = \frac{\log_{10} 8}{\log_{10} 2}$

6.13 Numerical Calculations – Practice Questions

1. A stack of 14 bricks is 28.42 inches tall. How tall is each brick?

    A. 397.88 inches

    B. 2.03 inches

    C. 0.49 inches

    D. 2.30 inches

    E. 2.02 inches

2. Which of the following fractions is the largest?

    A. $\frac{5}{7}$

    B. $\frac{9}{20}$

    C. $\frac{3}{5}$

    D. $\frac{5}{14}$

    E. $\frac{2}{3}$

3. A class of 25 students averaged an 84 on a quiz (out of 100). How many students would need to correctly do the 10-point extra credit to bring the average up to a 90?

    A. 15

    B. 10

    C. 12

    D. 8

    E. 11

4. Ashley buys 6 pears for $2 a pear, and 10 oranges for $1 per orange. What is the average price per fruit of the fruits Ashley bought?

    A. $1.00

    B. $1.25

    C. $1.52

    D. $2.00

    E. $1.38

5. It takes 35 minutes to clean 7/8 of a kitchen. How long does it take to clean the entire kitchen?

    A. 45 minutes

    B. 42 minutes

    C. 40 minutes

    D. 50 minutes

    E. 43 minutes

6. ¼ added to 1/5 is 60% of what number?

    A. 3/4

    B. 1/2

    C. 1/4

    D. 2/3

    E. 2/7

7. What is the 32nd digit (to the right of the decimal point) of the repeating decimal 0.246824682468…?

    A. 2

    B. 4

    C. 6

    D. 8

    E. 0

8. An orange tree yielded 60 oranges in one harvest year. The following year was a particularly bad harvest, and the tree produced 25 oranges. What is the percent decrease between the two harvest years?

    A. 35%

    B. 140%

    C. 55%

    D. 50%

    E. 58.3%

9. Of the 15,000 undergraduate students graduating from UM this year, 20% are pre-med, and 6% of the pre-med students are entering dental school. How many pre- med students are entering dental school?

    A. 180

    B. 3000

    C. 3900

    D. 2100

    E. 210

10. 0.004% of 0.06 is what?

    A. 0.024

    B. 0.0024

    C. 0.00024

    D. 0.000024

    E. 0.0000024

11. The letter A is 40% of B, which is 40% of C, which is 40% of D, whose value is 200. What is the value of A?

    A. 12.8

    B. 1.28

    C. 0.128

    D. 128

    E. 0.0128

12. 35% of what number is 21?

    A. 65

    B. 60

    C. 55

    D. 45

    E. 47

13. $\frac{2}{3}$% of 15 is?

    A. 1

    B. 0.01

    C. 0.1

    D. 10

    E. 0.001

14. Round to the next integer: $log_3 600$

    A. 2

    B. 3

    C. 4

    D. 5

    E. 6

15. Approximate $\sqrt{\sqrt{90,000}}$?

    A. 30

    B. 17

    C. 10

    D. 12

    E. 13

16. Express $(3 \times 10^4)^3$ in scientific notation?

    A. 3×10^7

    B. 3×10^{12}

    C. 2.7×10^{13}

    D. 27×10^{12}

    E. 2.7×10^7

17. Determine $\frac{8 \times 10^{-6}}{4 \times 10^{-13}}$?

    A. 2×10^{-6}

    B. 2×10^6

    C. 2×10^{-19}

    D. 2×10^{-7}

    E. 2×10^7

18. Find the product of $(4 \times 10^{-3}) \times (7 \times 10^{-9})$ in scientific notation?

    A. 2.8×10^{-11}

    B. 2.8×10^{-12}

    C. 28×10^{-11}

    D. 2.8×10^{-6}

    E. 2.8×10^6

19. Determine $\sqrt[3]{4096}$

    A. 13

    B. 22

    C. 18

    D. 16

    E. 14

20. Simplify: $\frac{8^4 - 16^3}{2^8}$?

    A. 1

    B. 0

    C. 2

    D. -1

    E. 4

21. If x = -2 and y = 3, what is the value of $\frac{2x^3 - 4y}{3y}$?

    A. -28/9

    B. 28/9

    C. 33/4

    D. -33/4

    E. 25/3

6.2 Numerical Calculations – Solutions

1. **B.**

$$\frac{28.42 \text{ inches}}{14} = 2.03 \text{ inches}$$

2. **A.** The easiest way to compare fractions with a calculator is to convert them to decimals by dividing. 5/7 is approximately .71, which is the largest decimal choice.

3. **A.** First, find the total number of points necessary to have an average of 90:

$$90 \times 25 \text{ students} = 2250 \text{ points}$$

Next, find the total number of points scored by the class (not including extra credit):

$$84 \times 25 \text{ students} = 2100 \text{ points}$$

The point difference is 2250 – 2100 = 150 points. Since each extra credit is worth 10 points, $\frac{150}{10}$ = 15 students who would need to correctly do the extra credit to bring the average up to a 90.

4. **E.** Ashley spent 6 x 2 = $12 on pears, and 10 x 1 = $10 on oranges, for a total of $22 on 16 pieces of fruit.

$$\frac{22}{16} = 1.375, \text{ or approximately } \$1.38 \text{ per fruit}$$

5. **C.** Since it takes 35 minutes to clean $\frac{7}{8}$ of a kitchen, set up the following equation, using x as the amount of time needed to clean the entire kitchen:

$$\frac{7}{8}x = 35$$

$$x = 35\left(\frac{8}{7}\right)$$

$$x = 40 \text{ minutes}$$

6. **A.**

$$\frac{1}{4} + \frac{1}{5} = 0.60x$$

$$0.25 + 0.20 = 0.60x$$

$$0.45 = 0.60x$$

$$\frac{0.45}{0.60} = x$$

$$0.75 = \frac{3}{4} = x$$

7. **D.** The base unit of repetition is "2468". The base unit repeats every four digits, so to find the 32nd digit, we divide 32 by 4, and we get 8. Since there is no remainder, the answer is the 4th digit of the repeating unit, which is 8.

8. **E.** To find a percent of increase or decrease, use the following formula:

$$\text{Percent of change} = \frac{\text{difference}}{\text{original}} \times 100\%$$

$$\text{Percent of change} = \frac{60 - 25}{60} \times 100\% = 58.3\%$$

9. **A.**

First, find what is 20% of 15,000:

$$0.20 \times 15,000 = 3,000$$

Then, find what is 6% of 3000:

$$0.06 \times 3,000 = 180 \text{ students}$$

10. **E.** Translate the question into a math expression using the table in section 6.5:

$$\frac{0.004}{100} \text{ x } 0.06 = 0.0000024$$

Note that percent $= \frac{x}{100}$, and "of" means multiplication.

11. **A.** Translate the question into a math expression using the table in section 6.5:

$$0.4 \times 0.4 \times 0.4 \times 200 = 12.8$$

Note that 40% is equivalent to 0.4 (40/100).

12. **B.** Set up the equation: .35x = 21, and solve for x.

$$0.35x = 21$$
$$x = \frac{21}{0.35}$$
$$x = 60$$

13. **C.** Translate the question into a math expression using the table in section 6.5:

$$\frac{\frac{2}{3}}{100} \text{ x } 15 = \frac{2}{3x100} \text{ x } 15 = 0.1$$

14. **E.** Using the logarithm rules, we can write the expression as:

$$\log_3 600 = x$$
$$3^x = 600$$

Start estimating x, using the base 3, that is close to 600:

$$3^5 = 243$$
$$3^6 = 729$$

600 is much closer to 729 than to 243, so we will round up to 6.

15. **B.** If you were to recognize that 90,000 is a perfect square, it may make the problem a bit easier. The square root of 90,000 is 300 ($\sqrt{9 \ x \ 10^4} = 3$ x 10^2), so now the problem becomes $\sqrt{300}$:

$$\sqrt{300} = \sqrt{100 \times 3} = 10\sqrt{3}$$

You know that $\sqrt{3} = 1.73$ so the answer needs to be a little less than 20 (since 10x2 = 20). Also, by guessing and checking, $17^2 = 289$, which is the closest perfect square to 300 without going over.

16. **C.** To solve this problem, we must first simplify the given expression. Everything in parentheses needs to be raised to the 3[rd.] power:

$$3^3 \times (10^4)^3$$

When raising a power to a power, you multiply the powers:

$$3^3 \times 10^{12}$$

Simplifying we get: 27 x 10^{12}

A number in scientific notation needs to be greater than 1, but less than 10, multiplied by 10 to a power. Since 27 is not in scientific notation, you will need to move the decimal to the left, turning the number into 2.7. Now it is a number greater than 1, but less than 10.

A trick is remembering the mnemonic MR. AL, which stands for "minus right, add left." Since we moved the decimal once to the left to make 27 into 2.7, you must add 1 to the exponent.

17. **E.** When dividing in scientific notation, divide the first numbers of each expression (in this case, it would be $\frac{8}{4} = 2$). Then the rules for dividing exponents when the bases are the same, is to keep the base and subtract the exponents. Therefore, you keep the 10 and calculate $-6 - (-13) = -6 + 13 = 7$

18. **A.** Multiplying 4 x 7 = 28. Multiplying 10^{-3} x 10^{-9}, keep the base and add the exponents = 10^{-12}. Since 28 is not a number greater than 1, but less than 10, you must move the decimal once to the right making it 2.8. Because you moved it once to the left, add 1 to your exponent. $-12 + 1 = -11$.

19. **D.** Because the DAT calculator does not have an exponent or a root key, the easiest way to solve this problem is to guess and check each answer choice by multiplying it times itself 3 times until you get 4096.

$$(16)(16)(16) = 4096$$

20. **B.** The first step is to convert the bases in the numerator to a base of 2, to match the denominator:

$$\frac{8^4 - 16^3}{2^8}$$

$$\frac{(2^3)^4 - (2^4)^3}{2^8}$$

$$\frac{2^{12} - 2^{12}}{2^8}$$

$$\frac{0}{2^8} = 0$$

21. **A.** Plug-in the given values for x and y into the given expression $\frac{2x^3 - 4y}{3y}$

$$\frac{2(-2^3) - 4(3)}{3(3)} = \frac{2(-8) - 4(3)}{3(3)} = \frac{-16 - 12}{9} = \frac{-28}{9}$$

Chapter 7: Trigonometry

This section is "technically" no longer on the DAT, yet it may be included in the quantitative comparison section, and thus, we still teach it in our course.

1. **Be familiar with the following trigonometric functions:**

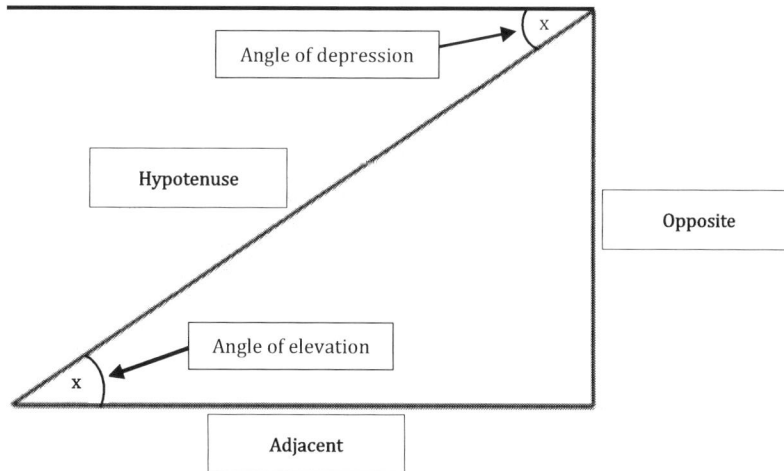

$$\sin \theta = \frac{Opposite}{Hypotenuse} \qquad \cos \theta = \frac{Adjacent}{Hypotenuse} \qquad \tan \theta = \frac{Opposite}{Adjacent}$$

- **Adjacent** is always next to the angle, and **Opposite** is opposite the angle
- Use arctan/ arcsine/arccos when you know the tangent/sine/cosine of an angle and want to know the actual angle

2. The **Law of Sines** (for non-right triangles): $\frac{Sin\ A}{a} = \frac{Sin\ B}{b} = \frac{Sin\ C}{c}$

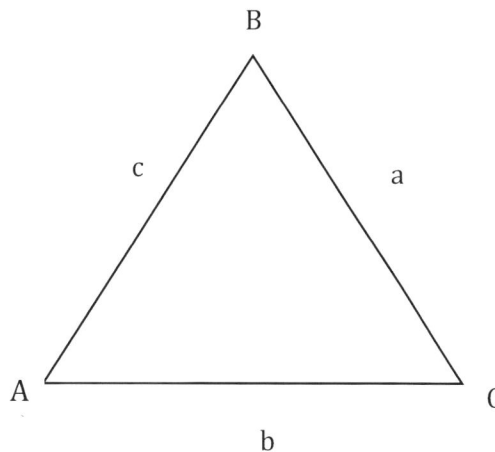

7.1 Trigonometry – Practice Questions

1. Matthew is looking through his office window that is 15 feet high above the ground. He looks down to see a dog that is sitting 8 feet away from the office building. Which of the followings is the angle of elevation from the dog to Matthew?

   A. $\text{Arctan}\left(\frac{15}{8}\right)$

   B. $\text{Arctan}\left(\frac{8}{15}\right)$

   C. $\text{Arccos}\left(\frac{15}{8}\right)$

   D. $\text{Arccos}\left(\frac{8}{15}\right)$

   E. $\text{Arcsin}\left(\frac{15}{8}\right)$

2. A rehabilitation center is building a ramp to the main door for their patients. What is the length of the ramp if the door is 5 ft above ground level, and the angle of elevation is 30°?

   A. $x = \frac{5}{\tan 30°}$

   B. $x = \frac{5}{\cos 30°}$

   C. $x = \frac{5}{\sin 30°}$

   D. $x = \frac{\sin 30°}{5}$

   E. $x = \frac{\tan 30°}{5}$

3. Which of the following is the value of side A?

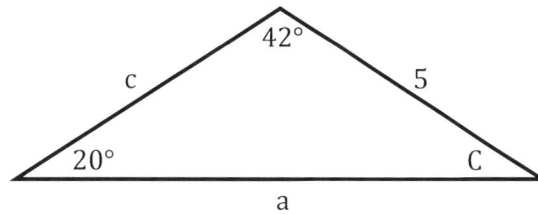

A. $\dfrac{(\sin 42°)(5)}{\sin 20°}$

B. $\dfrac{(\sin 20°)(5)}{\sin 42°}$

C. $\dfrac{(\cos 42°)(5)}{\cos 20°}$

D. $\dfrac{(\tan 42°)(5)}{\tan 20°}$

E. None of the above

7.2 Trigonometry – Solution

1. **A**

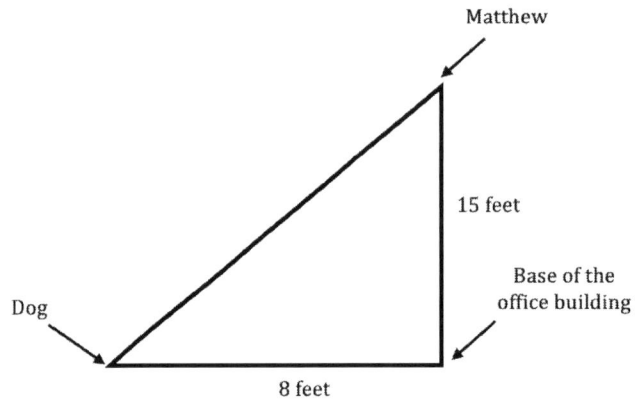

To answer this question, use the trig function tangent:

$$\text{Angle of elevation} = \frac{\text{Opposite}}{\text{Adjacent}}$$

$$\tan(x) = \frac{15}{8}$$

$$x = \text{Arctan}\left(\frac{15}{8}\right)$$

2. C

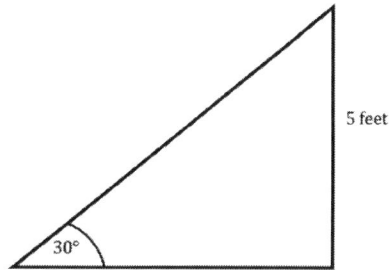

To answer this question, use the trig function sine (opposite/hypotenuse)

$$\sin 30° = \frac{5}{x} \text{ (cross multiply)}$$

$$x \sin 30° = 5$$

$$x = \frac{5}{\sin 30°}$$

3. A

Use the law of sines to set- up a proportion:

$$\frac{\sin A}{a} = \frac{\sin B}{b} = \frac{\sin C}{c}$$

$$\frac{\sin 42°}{a} = \frac{\sin 20°}{5}$$

Cross multiply:

$$(\sin 42°)(5) = (a)(\sin 20°)$$

Divide both sides by sin 20°:

$$\frac{(\sin 42°)(5)}{\sin 20°} = a$$

Chapter 8: Algebra

8.1 Arithmetic Operations

1. $ab + ac = a(b + c)$

2. $\dfrac{\left(\frac{a}{b}\right)}{c} = \dfrac{a}{bc}$

3. $a\left(\dfrac{b}{c}\right) = \dfrac{ab}{c}$

4. $\dfrac{a}{\left(\frac{b}{c}\right)} = \dfrac{ac}{b}$

5. $\dfrac{a}{b} + \dfrac{c}{d} = \dfrac{ad+bc}{bd}$

6. $\dfrac{a}{b} - \dfrac{c}{d} = \dfrac{ad-bc}{bd}$

7. $\dfrac{a+b}{c} = \dfrac{a}{c} + \dfrac{b}{c}$

8. $\dfrac{a-b}{c-d} = \dfrac{b-a}{d-c}$

9. $\dfrac{ab}{a} = b + c \qquad a \neq 0$

Sum of Arithmetic Sequence Formula	
When the Last Term is Given	$S = \dfrac{n}{2}(a + L)$
When the Last Term is Not Given	$S = \dfrac{n}{2}\{2a + (n - 1)d\}$

Notations
- "S" is the sum of the arithmetic sequence
- "a" is the first term
- "d" the common difference between the terms
- "n" is the total number of terms in the sequence
- "L" is the last term of the sequence

Example:

Find the sum of the first 30 terms of the sequence 5, 7, 9, 11, 13 …

Solution:

$$S = \frac{n}{2}\{2a + (n-1)d\}$$

$$S = \frac{30}{2}\{2(5) + (30-1)2\}$$

$$S = \frac{30}{2}\{10 + (29)2\}$$

$$S = \frac{30}{2}\{10 + 58\}$$

$$S = \frac{30}{2}\{68\}$$

$$S = 1020$$

8.2 Order of Operations

Parentheses > Exponents> Multiplication > Division > Addition > Subtraction

Mnemonic: Please **E**xcuse **M**y **D**ear **A**unt **S**andra **(PEMADS)**

Examples:

1. $6(8\text{-}2) + 4 = 6 \times 6 + 4 = 36 + 4 = 40$

2. $4 \times 5 + 6 \times 2 = 20 + 12 = 32$

8.3 Basic Rules of Multiplication and Division

Pay attention to the signs when you multiply and divide. There are two simple rules to remember:

- The **multiplication or division of two numbers with the same sign** (both negative or both positive) **results in a positive sign.**

Examples:

1. $(-3)(-2) = 6$
2. $(12)(3) = 36$

- The **multiplication or division of two numbers with different sign** (one negative and one positive) **results in a negative sign.**

Examples:

1. $(-3)(2) = -6$
2. $(-6)/(3) = -2$

Multiplication and Division with Exponents

▪ $a^m \times a^n = a^{m+n}$	▪ $a^m \div a^n = a^{m-n}$
▪ $a^m \times b^m = (a \times b)^m$	▪ $a^m \div b^m = (a \div b)^m$

DAT TIP: When **multiplying exponents with a common base, add the exponents.** When **dividing exponents with a common base, subtract the exponents.**

Divisibility Rules

A number is said to **be evenly divisible by another if the result of the division is an integer with no remainder**. A number that is evenly divisible by a second number is also a multiple of the second number.

For example, $52 \div 4 = 13$, which is an integer. Therefore 52 is evenly divisible by 4, and it's also a multiple of 4.

- An integer is **divisible by 2 if its last digit is even**
- An integer is **divisible by 3 if the sum of digits is divisible 3**
- An integer is **divisible by 4 if its last two digits are a multiple of 4**
- An integer is **divisible by 5 if its last digit is 0 or 5**
- An integer is **divisible by 6 if is divisible by 2 and 3**
- An integer is **divisible by 9 if the sum of digits is divisible 9**
- An integer is **divisible by 10 of its last digit is 0**

8.4 Absolute Value

The absolute value is **the distance of the number from zero on a number line**. Therefore, whether the number inside the two vertical lines is positive or negative, **the value is always positive.**

- $|a| = |-a| = a$
- $|a| \geq 0$
- $|a + b| = |a| + |b|$

- $|ab| = |a||b|$
- $\left|\dfrac{a}{b}\right| = \dfrac{|a|}{|b|}$

Examples:

$|5| = |-5| = 5$

$|3 + 4| = |3| + |4|$

$|3 \times 4| = |3| \times |4|$

$\left|\dfrac{4}{3}\right| = \dfrac{|4|}{|3|}$

8.5 Properties of Zero

1. The addition or subtraction of zero does not change the number (i.e., $5+0 = 5$)
2. Subtracting a number from zero results in a negative sign (i.e., $0-5 = -5$)
3. The multiplication of zero by any number (positive or negative) equals zero ($0 \times 5 = 0$)
4. **The division of any number (positive or negative) by zero is undefined** (cannot be done)

8.6 Odd/ Even Numbers

Even numbers **are divisive** by 2, **whereas** odd numbers **are** not evenly divisible by 2. **Note that zero is an even number.**

Integers that their **last digit** is **0,2,4,6 or 8 are even**

Integers that their **last digit** is **1,3,5,7, or 9 are odd**

Rules of odds/even integers

Odd + Odd = Even	Odd x Odd = Odd
Even + Even = Even	Even x Even = Even
Odd + Even = Odd	Odd x Even = Even

8.7 Factors and Prime Numbers

The **factors** of an integer are **all the positive integers by which it is evenly divisible (no remainder).** i.e., the factors of 24 are 1, 2, 3, 4, 6, 8, 12, and 24

The **greatest common factor (GCF) of two or more integers** is the **largest positive integer that divides each of the integers** (i.e., the GCF of 8 and 64 is 8)

A **prime number** is an integer **greater than 1 with only two factors – themselves and 1.** A prime number cannot be divided by any other number without leaving a reminder. 2 is the smallest, and the only even prime number.

The **prime numbers up to 100 are**:

2, 3, 5, 7, 11, 13, 17, 19, 23, 29, 31, 37, 41, 43, 47, 53, 59, 61, 67, 71, 73, 79, 83, 89 and 97

8.8 Factorial

The term n! is the product of **all the numbers beginning with n and counting backwards to 1**. We define 0! to be 1.

Examples:

$4! = 4 \times 3 \times 2 \times 1 = 24$

$5! = 5 \times 4 \times 3 \times 2 \times 1 = 120$

8.9 Factoring Formulas

1. $(x + y)^2 = (x + y)(x + y) = x^2 + 2xy + y^2$
2. $(x - y)^2 = (x - y)(x - y) = x^2 - 2xy + y^2$
3. $x^2 - y^2 = (x + y)(x - y)$
4. $x^2 + y^2 = (x + y)^2 - 2xy$
5. $x^3 + y^3 = (x + y)(x^2 - xy + y^2) = (x + y)^3 - 3xy(x + y)$
6. $x^3 - y^3 = (x - y)(x^2 + xy + y^2) = (x - y)^3 + 3xy(x - y)$

8.10 The Distance Between Two Points Formula

If $p_{1=}(x_1, y_1)$ and $p_{2=}(x_2, y_2)$ are two points, the distance between them is:

$$d = \sqrt{(x_2 - x_1)^2 + (y_2 - y_1)^2}$$

8.11 Slope – Intercept Form

$$y = mx + b$$

$m = $ slope and $b = $ y intercept of the line

8.12 Point – Slope Form

$$y - y_1 = m(x - x_1)$$

8.13 The Slope Formula

$$m = \frac{y_2 - y_1}{x_2 - x_1}$$

- **Parallel lines:** have the **same slope** (i.e., $y = x - \frac{1}{2}$ and $y = x + \frac{1}{2}$)
- **Perpendicular lines:** have **negative reciprocal slopes** (i.e., $y = x - \frac{1}{2}$ and $y = -x + \frac{1}{2}$)
- **Vertical line:** undefined slope
- **Horizontal line:** no slope

8.14 The Midpoint of a Line Segment Formula

$$(x, y) = (\frac{x_1 + x_2}{2} , \frac{x_1 + x_2}{2})$$

8.15 The Quadratic Equation

$$\text{For } ax^2 + bx + c = 0$$

$$x = \frac{-b \pm \sqrt{b^2 - 4ac}}{2a}$$

8.16 Rate of Depreciation / Appreciation

Appreciation

In situations, such as the growth of population/ bacteria, increase in the value of an asset etc., the following formula is used:

$$A = P(1 + \frac{r}{100})^n$$

Where **p** is the present value, **r** is the rate of increase, and **n** is the number of years.

Depreciation

In situation, where the cost of machines, vehicles, value of some articles etc. decreases, the following formula is used:

$$D = P(1 - \frac{r}{100})^n$$

Where **p** is the present value, **r** is the rate of decrease, and **n** is the number of years.

8.17 Age Problems

1. Write the people's names in columns (one column for each)

2. Give the youngest person the value x

3. For the other people in the question, assign an age in reference to x (i.e., four years older x+4)

4. Set up an equation between two people so that the two sides of the equation are equal by adding, subtracting, or multiplying one of the sides. Note that the smaller side will be added the difference (i.e., if the smaller side is 4 less, add to it 4 to be equal to the larger side)

5. Solve

Example:

Sara is 35 years old. Three years ago, Sara was four times as old as Nicole then. How old is Nicole now?

	Sara		Nicole
Now:	35		x
3 years ago:	35-3		x-3
Set up equation:	35-3	=	4 (x-3)
Solve:	32	=	4x-12
		44 = 4x	
		x = 11	

> Sara is 4 times older, so I multiplied Nicole's age by 4 to make them equal

8.18 System of Equations

There are three ways to solve systems of linear equations: Substitution, Elimination, and Graphing.

Substitution

1. Isolate one of the variables in one of the equations

2. Take the expression you got for the variable in step 1 and plug it (substitute it by using parentheses) into the other equation.

3. Solve the equation in step 2 for the remaining variable.

4. Use the result from step 3 and plug it into the equation from step 1.

Substitution Example

$$\begin{cases} 2x + 5y = 19 \\ 2y = 6x - 6 \end{cases}$$

$$\begin{cases} 2x + 5y = 19 \\ 2y = 6x - 6 \ /2 \end{cases}$$

$$\begin{cases} 2x + 5y = 19 \\ y = 3x - 3 \end{cases} \longleftarrow$$ Substitute the 3x – 3 for y in equation 1

$$2x + 5 (3x - 3) = 19$$

$$2x + 15x - 15 = 19$$

$$17x = 34$$

$$x = 2$$

If x = 2, then we can plug in its value to any of the two equations to solve for y:

$$2y = 6(2)\text{-}6$$

$$2y = 12\text{-}6$$

$$2y = 6$$

$$y = 3$$

Elimination

1. If necessary, rearrange both equations so that the x-terms are first, followed by the y-terms, the equals sign, and the constant term (in that order). If an equation appears to have no constant term, that means that the constant term is 0.

2. Multiply one (or both) equations by a constant that will allow either the x-terms or the y-terms to cancel when the equations are added or subtracted (when their left sides and their right sides are added separately, or when their left sides and their right sides are subtracted separately).

3. Add or subtract the equations.

4. Solve for the remaining variable.

5. Plug the result of step 4 into one of the original equations and solve for the other variable.

Elimination Example

$$\begin{cases} 3x + 2y = 7 \\ 5x - 3y = 37 \end{cases}$$

$$\begin{cases} 3x + 2y = 7/(x3) \\ 5x - 3y = 37/(x2) \end{cases}$$

$$\begin{cases} 9x + 6y = 21 \\ 10x - 6y = 74 \end{cases}$$

$$19x = 95$$

$$x = 5$$

If x =5, then we can plug - in its value to any of the two equations to solve for y:

$$3(5) + 2y = 7$$

$$15 + 2y = 7$$

$$2y = -8$$

$$y = -4$$

Graphing

1. Solve for y in each equation

2. Graph both equations on the same Cartesian coordinate system

3. Find the point of intersection point of the lines (the point where the lines cross)

8.19 Inequalities

When you multiply or divide the inequality by a negative number, you must reverse the direction of the inequality. i.e., -4x < 2, and when divided by -1 we get: 4x > -2.

Rules:

- \> is greater than

- ≥ is greater than or equal to

- < is less than

- ≤ is less than or equal to

Examples:

$4x + 6 > 3x + 7$

$4x > 3x + 1$

$x > 1$

8.20 Solving inequalities with absolute value

$|x| < 5$ rewrite as $-5 < x < 5$

$|x| ≤ 5$ rewrite as $-5 ≤ x ≤ 5$

$|x + 5| < 25$ rewrite as $-25 < x + 5 < 25$

8.21 Graphs Interpretations

	Even power	Odd power
Positive constant $K > 0$		
Negative constant $K < 0$		

Parent Function

Constant	Linear	Absolute Value	Quadratic
$f(x)=c$	$f(x)=x$	$f(x)=|x|$	$f(x)=x^2$
Square Root	Cubic	Cube Root	Reciprocal/ Inverse/ Rational
$f(x)=\sqrt{x}$	$f(x)=x^3$	$f(x)=\sqrt[3]{x}$	$f(x)=\frac{1}{x}$
Rational	Logarithmic	Exponential	Greater Integer (Step Function)
$f(x)=\frac{1}{x^2}$	$f(x)=\ln(x)$	$f(x)=e^x$	$f(x)=[[x]]$
Trig Functions →	$f(x)=\sin(x)$	$f(x)=\cos(x)$	$f(x)=\tan(x)$

DAT TIP: When you are asked to determine the **system of inequalities of a region between two functions (curve or a line)**, first determine which function belongs to each curve or line and then decide if the shaded area is below (less than) or above (greater than) each curve/ line.

8.22 Symbolic Functions

Symbolic functions such as ◆ or ⊛ may appear in equations. Don't get overwhelmed. Just be attentive to the pattern in the equation and follow it.

Example:

If x ★ y = 2• x • 2 − 3y, what is the value of 4 ★ 2?

A. 2

B. 4

C. 8

D. 10

E. 12

In the example above, you get x ★ y and are asked to solve for 4 ★ 2. That means to replace **x** and **y** with **4** and **2**, respectively, and then do the arithmetic:

x ★ y = 2• x •2 − 3y

4 ★ 2 = 2(4)2 − 3(2)

4 ★ 2 = 16 − 6

4 ★ 2 = 10

So, the correct answer is (D).

8.23 Algebra – Practice Questions

1. Given $2x + 4y = -6$ and $6x - 4y = 4$, what is the value of x?

    A. $-11/8$

    B. $11/8$

    C. $-1/4$

    D. $7/6$

    E. $-3/4$

2. Which of the following is a possible value of x if $(-128x^2 - 1)^3 = -27$?

    A. $\frac{1}{64}$

    B. $\frac{1}{16}$

    C. $\frac{1}{8}$

    D. $\frac{1}{2}$

    E. $\frac{1}{128}$

3. Which of the following is equivalent to $(4x - 5y)^2$?

    A. $40(x - y)^2$

    B. $16x^2 + 25y^2$

    C. $16x^2 + 40xy + 25y^2$

    D. $16x^2 - 40xy - 25y^2$

    E. $16x^2 - 40xy + 25y^2$

4. Which of the following is a possible value of x if $\sqrt{-x^3 - 14} = 5\sqrt{2}$?

   A. 4

   B. ¼

   C. -5

   D. 5

   E. -4

5. Which of the following is closely equivalent to $x^2 + 4x - 21 / x^2 - 9$?

   A. $(x - 7) / (x + 3)$

   B. $(x + 7) / (x - 3)$

   C. $(x + 7) / (x^2 - 9)$

   D. $(x - 3) / (x + 3)$

   E. $(x + 7) / (x + 3)$

6. If $\frac{6}{x^2 - 9} \times \frac{x+3}{4} = 8$, then what is the value of x?

   A. 51/16

   B. 3/2

   C. 1/16

   D. 4/5

   E. 1/3

7. If $(x + y)^4 = (x - y)^2 = 81$, then what is the value of x?

   A. 13/2

   B. 9

   C. 3

   D. 6

   E. 5/3

8. At what point does the following pair of lines intersect?

$$-x + 2y = 25$$

$$x + 5y = 10$$

   A. (5, -15)

   B. (-15, 5)

   C. (5, 15)

   D. (-15, -5)

   E. (0, -5)

9. Which of the following is the equation of the line that contains the point (3, -2) and is perpendicular to the line $y = -3x + 4$?

   A. $y = -3x - 3$

   B. $y = 3x - 3$

   C. $y = -1/3x - 3$

   D. $y = 1/3x - 3$

   E. $y = 1/3x + 3$

10. For which values of x is the function f(x) undefined if $f(x) = \frac{x+2}{x^2-4}$?

    A. $x = 2$

    B. $x = -2$

    C. $x = 4$

    D. $x = 2$ and $x = -2$

    E. $x = 0$

11. If $x + y = 2$ and $4a + 4b = 24$, then which of the following is equivalent to:

$$(x+y)^3 \div (a+b)?$$

    A. 4

    B. 3

    C. 4/3

    D. 2/3

    E. 6

12. Mike is only 5 years older than his brother Tim. 13 years ago, Mike was 6 years short of being twice Tim's age. How old is Tim now?

    A. 21

    B. 22

    C. 23

    D. 24

    E. 25

13. Molly's age is 2 more than twice Amy's age. In 4 years, Molly will be 3 times as old as Amy is now. How old is Molly?

13. Molly's age is 2 more than twice Amy's age. In 4 years, Molly will be 3 times as old as Amy is now. How old is Molly?

    A. 14

    B. 6

    C. 12

    D. 10

    E. 13

14. Which of the following is a solution to this system of inequalities?

$$(x + 2)^2 > 1$$

$$|x + 3| > 1$$

    A. -4

    B. -3

    C. -2

    D. -1

    E. 0

15. If $27^{4m + 5} = 3^{3m + 18}$, then what is the value of m?

    A. 3

    B. 5/6

    C. 1/3

    D. 6/5

    E. 2

16. There are 15 boys in an algebra class that also contains girls. The ratio of girls to boys is 4 to 3. How many girls are there in the algebra class?

    A. 20

    B. 15

    C. 25

    D. 30

    E. 10

17. A car can travel 480 miles in 8 hours. How long will it take to travel 900 miles?

    A. 12 hours

    B. 10 hours

    C. 15 hours

    D. 13 hours

    E. 20 hours

18. Which expression best represents the shaded portion of the graph below?

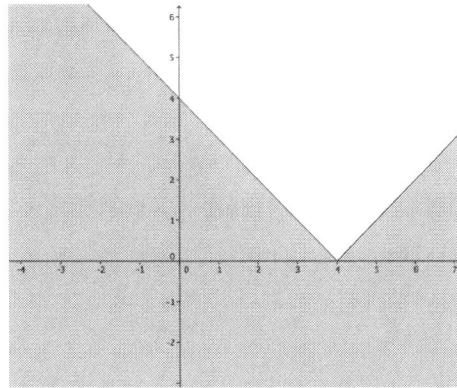

A. $y \leq x - 4$

B. $y \leq x + 4$

C. $y \geq x - 4$

D. $y \leq |x - 4|$

E. $y \leq |x - 5|$

19. Which of the following inequalities corresponds to the graph shown?

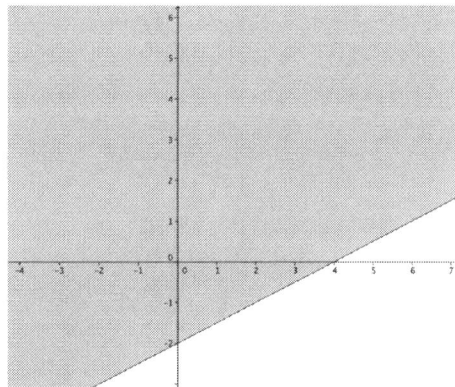

A. $y = 4x$

B. $y \leq x - 4$

C. $4y \geq 2x - 8$

D. $y \geq 4x$

E. $3y \leq 2x - 3$

20. Solve the inequality: $|5 - x| < 16$

    A. $x > -11$

    B. $x < 21$

    C. $x < -11$ and $x > 21$

    D. $-11 < x < 21$

    E. $x < -11$

21. Find the solution set for $|3x - 4| \leq 16$

    A. $-4 \leq x$ and $x \geq 20/3$

    B. $x \leq -4$ and $x \geq 20/3$

    C. $-4 \leq x \leq 20/3$

    D. $x \leq -4$ or $x \geq 20/3$

    E. $-4 \leq x$ or $x \leq 20/3$

8.24 Algebra – Solutions

1. **C.** This problem can be solved using a linear system of equations. There are 2 algebraic methods for solving linear systems: elimination and substitution. Elimination involves cancelling out one variable to solve for the other. In this case, we can eliminate the y variable to solve for x.

$$2x + 4y = -6$$

$$6x - 4y = 4$$

Adding these together results in:

$$8x = -2$$

$$x = \frac{-2}{8} = \frac{-1}{4}$$

2. **C.** The first step in solving this equation is to cancel out the 3rd power around the parentheses, which requires taking the cube root of both sides:

$(-128x^2 - 1)^3 = -27$ Take the cube root of both sides

$-128x^2 - 1 = -3$ Add 1 to both sides

$-128x^2 = -2$ Divide both sides by -128

$$x^2 = \frac{1}{64}$$
$$x = \frac{1}{8}$$

Also, note that there will always be a positive and negative root when taking a square root, so $-\frac{1}{8}$ would have also been a valid answer.

3. **E.** One way to solve this equation is to multiply the binomial by itself $(4x - 5y)$ $(4x - 5y)$ and simplify:

$$(4x - 5y)\ (4x - 5y)$$

$$16x^2 - 20xy - 20xy + 25y^2$$

$$16x^2 - 40xy + 25y^2$$

A shortcut for multiplying binomials is to

1. Square the first term $(4x)(4x) = 16x^2$

2. Multiply the terms together and then multiply by 2.

$$(4x)(5y) = 20xy \times 2 = 40xy$$

3. Square the second term $(5y)(5y) = 25y^2$

    Put it together: $16x^2 - 40xy + 25y^2$

4. **E.** To start solving, square both sides:

$$\sqrt{-x^3 - 14} = 5\sqrt{2}$$

$$-x^3 - 14 = 50$$

$$-x^3 = 64$$

$$x^3 = -64$$

$$x = -4$$

Note that a way to cancel out a square root is to square both sides of the equation. The square cancels out the square root.

5. **E.** Factor and simplify the following expression:

$$\frac{x^2 + 4x - 21}{x^2 - 9}$$

$$\frac{(x + 7)(x - 3)}{(x + 3)(x - 3)}$$

$$\frac{(x + 7)}{(x + 3)}$$

6. **A.**

$$\frac{6}{x^2-9} \times \frac{x+3}{4} = 8$$ To start, factor x²-9

$$\frac{6}{(x+3)(x-3)} \times \frac{x+3}{4} = 8$$ (x+3) on the numerator and denominator cancels out

$$\frac{6}{x-3} \times \frac{1}{4} = 8$$ Multiply the fractions

$$\frac{6}{4(x-3)} = 8$$ Distribute

$$\frac{6}{4x-12} = 8$$ Cross multiply

$$8(4x-12) = 6$$ Distribute and solve

$$32x - 96 = 6$$

$$32x = 102$$

$$x = 51/16$$

7. **D.**

$$(x + y)^4 = (x - y)^2 = 81$$

To solve this problem, separate the expressions and set them each equal to 81

$$(x + y)^4 = 81 \qquad \text{and} \qquad (x - y)^2 = 81$$

Take the 4th root of the first equation, and the square root of the second equation:

$$x + y = 3 \qquad \text{and} \qquad x - y = 9$$

Combine both equations, so that the y terms cancel out:

$$x + y = 3$$
$$x - y = 9$$

Therefore:

$$2x = 12$$

$$x = 6$$

8. **B.** You could plug-in every answer choice into BOTH equations, until you find the answer that satisfies both equations, or you can use the elimination method. Using elimination, the x's cancel out:

$$-x + 2y = 25$$

$$x + 5y = 10$$

Next, combine like terms going down vertically:

$$7y = 35$$
$$y = 5$$

Plug -in 5 back in for y to either equation gives you -15 for x. Therefore, the answer is (-15, 5).

9. **D.** Perpendicular lines have opposite sign, reciprocal slopes. Therefore, a line perpendicular to the line y = -3x +4 would have a slope of 1/3. This narrows the choices down to D or E. The easiest thing to do would be to then plug-in the given point of (3, -2) into both equations and see which one satisfies the equation. In choice [D] this would be -2 = 1/3(3) – 3 which is true.

10. **D.** It is tempting to factor the denominator x^2 – 4 and cancel out the factors (x+2) to yield the expressions $\frac{1}{x-2}$, which is undefined for x = 2 alone. But this procedure eliminates one of the two discontinuities present in the original function. If you plug in 2 or -2 to the original equation for x, $\frac{x+2}{x^2-4}$ both would make the denominator = 0, which makes the function undefined.

11. **C.** If 4a + 4b = 24, then dividing the equation by 4 means that a + b = 6. Since x + y = 2, we can substitute 2 into the expression, along with substituting in 6 for a+b.

$$(x+y)^3 \div (a+b)$$

$$(2)^3 \div (6)$$

$$8 \div 6 = \frac{4}{3}$$

12. **D.**

M	T	
x + 5	x	(Mike is 5 years older than Tim)
x + 5 - 13	x-13	(13 years ago)
x + 5 - 13 + 6 = (x -13)2		Mike is 6 less than twice Tim, so to make them equal, I added 6 to Mike

$$x-2 = 2x-26$$

$$-x = -24$$

$$x = 24$$

13. **A.**

M	A	
2 + 2x	x	(Molly is 2 more than twice Amy)
+4		(in 4 years)
6+2x =	3x	(Molly is 3 times Amy NOW)

$$x = 6$$

14. **E.** The easiest way to solve this problem would be to plug-in each answer choice into BOTH inequalities, until you find the number which makes them both true.

$$(0 + 2)^2 > 1 \quad 2^2 > 1 \quad TRUE$$

$$|0 + 3| > 1 \quad 3 > 1 \quad TRUE$$

15. **C.** First, rename 27^{4m+5} so that it has a base of 3: $(3^3)^{4m+5}$

According to exponent rules, keep the base of 3 and multiply the exponents:

$$(3^3)^{4m+5} = 3^{12m+15}$$

Now, this expression and 3^{3m+18} have the same base, so **if the bases are equal then the exponents must be equal.**

$$12m + 15 = 3m + 18$$

$$9m + 15 = 18$$

$$9m = 3$$

$$m = 1/3$$

16. **A.** First, if the ratio of girls to boys is 4 to 3, this means there are more girls in the class than boys. Since there are 15 boys in the class, this narrows the choices down to [A],[C], or [D]. You can then set-up a proportion to find the number of girls:

$$\frac{4 \text{ girls}}{3 \text{ boys}} = \frac{x \text{ girls}}{15 \text{ boys}}$$

Next, cross multiply: $3x = 60$, so $x = 20$, or you can see that the number of boys is 5 times as much, therefore the number of girls would be 5 times as much. $4(5) = 20$

17. **C.** This problem can be solved using a proportion. Then, cross-multiply to solve.

$$\frac{480 \text{ miles}}{8 \text{ hours}} = \frac{900 \text{ miles}}{x \text{ hours}}$$

$$900(8) = 480x$$

$$7200 = 480x$$

$$x = 15$$

18. **D.** You can tell by the **V-shape** of the graph that this is an **absolute value inequality**. Plugging - in values (such as point 4,0) shows that the answer is D.

19. **C.** Isolate y by dividing all terms by 4, gives an inequality of $y \geq 1/2x - 2$, which is the line graphed. Since it is greater than or equal to, the shading should be above the line.

20. **D.** To solve this absolute value inequality, we should start by writing it as a combined inequality that accounts for both positive and negative cases:

$|5 - x| < 16$

$-16 < 5 - x < 16$ Solve for x by subtracting 5 from both sides, then dividing by -1

$-21 < -x < 11$

$21 > x > -11$

**When dividing or multiplying an inequality with a negative number, the inequality signs must be flipped: $21 > x > -11$, which can be reordered as $-11 < x < 21$, the correct answer.

21. **C.** When absolute value is less than or equal to a given value, this is an "and" inequality:

$$|3x - 4| \leq 16$$
$$-16 \leq 3x - 4 \leq 16$$
$$-12 \leq 3x \leq 20$$
$$-4 \leq x \leq 20/3$$

Chapter 9: Applied Mathematics

Applied mathematics consists of word problems. Below are tips for solving word problems on the DAT:

9.1 Plug – in numbers

- Used for problems with variables in the question and in the answer choices
- Choose simple numbers (easily divisible and multiplied) for each variable

9.2 Interest formulas

Simple Interest

$$I = PRT$$

- **I** = Interest
- **P** = Initial value
- **R** = Interest rate
- **T** = time (years)

Compound Interest Annually

$$A = P(1 + r)^t$$

- **A** = future value
- **P** = original value
- **r** = interest rate (in decimal form)
- **t** = number of years compounded

Example: What is the future value of a portfolio worth $100 earning 5% compounded annually after 20 years?

$$A = P\,(1 + r)^t$$
$$A = 100\,(1 + 0.05)^{20}$$
$$A = \$265$$

Compound Interest Monthly

$$A = P\,(1 + \frac{r}{n})^{nt}$$

- **A** = future value
- **P** = original value
- **r** = interest rate (in decimal form)
- **n** = number of times that the interest rate is compounded per year
- **t** = number of years compounded

Example: Cynthia deposits $2,350 in an account that earns interest at a rate of 3.1%, compounded monthly. What is her ending balance after 5 years?

$$A = P\,(1 + \frac{r}{n})^{nt}$$
$$A = \$2{,}350\left(1 + \frac{0.031}{12}\right)^{12 \cdot 5}$$
$$A = \$2{,}743.45$$

9.3 The Distance Formula

$$\text{Distance} = \text{Rate x Time}$$

$$D = R \text{ x } T$$

$$\text{Average speed} = \frac{\text{Total Distance}}{\text{Total Time}}$$

- **D** = distance
- **R** = rate/ speed
- **T** = time

Example:

A truck traveling at an average speed of 50 kilometers per hour made a trip to town in 6 hours. If it had traveled at 45 kilometers per hour, how many more minutes would it have taken to make the trip?

At 50 km/hour, the truck traveled: 50 km/hr. x 6 hours = 300 km

Since the distance traveled in both cases is the same, we get the equation:

$$45t = 300$$

$$t = \frac{300}{45} = 6\frac{2}{3}$$

Note the question asked for "how many more minutes", so we need to deduct the original 6 hours taken:

$$6\frac{2}{3} - 6 = \frac{2}{3} \text{ hours} = 40 \text{ minutes}$$

Therefore, the time taken would have been 40 minutes longer.

9.4 Upstream/ Downstream Rate Problems

- **Stream:** the movement of water in a river

- **Upstream:** when the **boat** is flowing in the **opposite direction to the stream**

- **Downstream:** when the **boat** is flowing **along the direction of the stream**

- **Still water:** under this circumstance the water is stationary, and the **speed of the water is zero**

- **Upstream = (u−v)** where "u" is the speed of the boat in still water and "v" is the speed of the stream

- **Downstream = (u+v)** where "u" is the speed of the boat in still water and "v" is the speed of the stream

Example:

Ron drives his boat downstream at a speed of 13 km/hr. If the speed of the stream is 4 km/hr., then how long would it take Ron to boat 68 km downstream?

Solution:

Downstream speed = (13+4) km/hr. = 17 km/hr.

Therefore, to travel 68 km downstream: 68/17 = 4 hours

9.5 The Combined Work Formula

$$\frac{1}{T_1} + \frac{1}{T_2} + \frac{1}{T_3} + \ldots = \frac{T_1 T_2 T_3}{T_1 + T_2 + T_3} = \frac{1}{T_{Total}}$$

Note that T_1 is the time taken by the 1st person, T_2 by the second person, etc.

Example: If it takes Ron 3 hours, and Michael 4 hours to fold the same laundry, how long would it take them to fold the laundry together?

$$\frac{1}{3} + \frac{1}{4} = \frac{7}{12} = \frac{1}{T_{Total}}$$

$$7T = 12$$

$$T = 1.71 \text{ hours}$$

9.6 The Average Formula

$$\text{Avg.} = \frac{\text{Total Sum of All Terms}}{\text{Number of Terms}}$$

9.7 Proportions/ Ratios

A proportion is **a statement that two ratios are equal**. It can be written in two ways: as two equal fractions $a/b = c/d$; or using a colon, $a:b = c:d$.

In problems involving proportions, we can **use cross-multiplication to find a missing term in a proportion.** To find the cross products of a proportion, we multiply the outer terms, the extremes, the middle terms, and the means.

Example:

If the ratio of girls to boys is 3:5, then how many boys are in a class of 15 girls?

$$\frac{3}{5} \bowtie \frac{15}{x}$$

$$3x = 15 \times 5$$

$$3x = 75$$

$$x = 25$$

9.8 Coin Word Problems

Coin problems are a category of word problems that **involve pennies, nickels, dimes, quarters, or half dollars.**

Example: **Rana bought a notebook and received change for $3 in 20 coins, all nickels, and quarters. How many of each coin did Rana get?**

Let:

n = number of nickels

q = number of quarters

Total = quantity × value

n + q = 20   (equation 1)

5n + 25q = 300   (equation 2)

* Note that we multiplied equation 2 by 100 so that nickel = 5 rather than 0.05 and the quarter = 25 rather than 0.25.

Use substitution method to isolate n in equation 1:

n = 20 – q   (equation 3)

Substitute equation 3 into equation 2:

5(20 – q) + 25q = 300

100 – 5q + 25q = 300

25q – 5q = 300 – 100

20q = 200

q = 10

Substitute q = 10 into equation 1:

n + 10 = 20

n = 10

Rana received 10 nickels and 10 quarters.

9.9 Applied Mathematics – Practice Questions

1. Matt, Nicole, and Connor each went running. Matt ran m miles, and Nicole ran 4 miles less than Matt. If Connor ran 2 miles less than double what Nicole ran, how far did Connor run?

    A. $2m - 4$

    B. $2m - 2$

    C. $2(m-4)$

    D. $2m - 4 - 2$

    E. $2(m-4) - 2$

2. A homeowner wants to put in new tile in his living room. The shape must be a square, and it needs to have an area of 275 feet². What is the minimum length of each side of the square?

    A. 14 ft.

    B. 15 ft.

    C. 16 ft.

    D. 17 ft.

    E. 18 ft.

3. The price of a gallon of milk typically increases at a rate of 3% per year. If a gallon of milk costs $2.49 in the year 2016, how much would you expect it to cost in the year 2020?

    A. $2.55

    B. $2.62

    C. $2.76

    D. $2.80

    E. $2.89

4. Jackie makes a 50-mile trip. She drives the first 25 miles at a speed of 50 miles per hour, and the second 25 miles at a speed of 30 miles per hour. What is Jackie's average speed for the entire 50-mile trip?

   A. 35 mph

   B. 36 mph

   C. 36.5 mph

   D. 37.5 mph

   E. 37 mph

5. A boy band is paid an 8 percent royalty on gross sales of their new album on iTunes, with a $20,000 advance against royalties. If the album sells for $12.99 on iTunes, and there are 35,000 downloads, approximately, how much in royalties, after the initial $20,000 advance, does the boy band earn?

   A. $40,586

   B. $16,285

   C. $36,372

   D. $454,650

   E. $16,372

6. Gear A and Gear B have equally sized and spaced teeth that mesh so that when one gear turns, the other is also forced to turn without slipping. Gear A has 10 teeth, and Gear B has 20 teeth. If Gear A turns 30 times, how many times does Gear B turn?

   A. 10

   B. 12

   C. 15

   D. 20

   E. 30

7. A truck depreciates 25% each year. The truck's value at the end of three years is $10,264. What was the approximate initial value of the truck?

   A. $25,857

   B. $21,235

   C. $22,948

   D. $24,329

   E. $23,485

8. Adam orders 500 baseball cards for a total of $1000. If 10% of the cards get damaged during shipping and are unsellable, what should Adam charge per card to make a 200% profit?

   A. $5.23

   B. $6.67

   C. $4.75

   D. $3.39

   E. $2.99

9. Harper took 4 courses at UM this past semester. She earned a B in chemistry (4 credits), an A in a chemistry lab (1 credit), an A in Calculus (3 credits), and a C in Calculus Lab (1 credit). If grades are weighted such that an A is four grade points, a B is three grades points, and a C is two grade points, what is Harper's grade point average from this past semester?

   A. 3.12

   B. 3.54

   C. 3.25

   D. 3.67

   E. 3.33

10. Andy can paint a wall in 2 hours, while Brad can paint the same size wall in 3 hours. If they work together, and charge $50 an hour, how much should they charge to paint 4 walls?

    A. $285

    B. $260

    C. $200

    D. $210

    E. $240

11. 4 liters of 40% iodine solution is mixed with 8 liters of 12% solution. What is the percent of iodine in the mixture?

    A. 19.8%

    B. 23.4%

    C. 21.3%

    D. 26.7%

    E. 25.9%

12. A bus can travel 100 miles in two hours. How many miles can it travel in 9 hours?

    A. 375

    B. 300

    C. 450

    D. 400

    E. 500

13. Andy can paint a wall in 6 hours, while Brad can paint the same wall in 5 hours. If Andy paints the wall for 3 hours, how much time will it take Brad to finish painting the same wall?

    A. 1 hr.

    B. 1.5 hrs.

    C. 2 hrs.

    D. 3 hrs.

    E. 2.5 hrs.

14. A box of cookies normally costs $3. If there is a sale to get 15 boxes of cookies for the price of $15, what is the price per box, considering a 6% sales tax?

    A. $2.12

    B. $6.00

    C. $1.06

    D. $1.77

    E. $1.82

15. Megan has a total of 15 coins in quarters, dimes, and nickels. Their total worth is $2.20. If Megan has 4 nickels, how many dimes does she have?

    A. 8
    B. 4
    C. 6
    D. 5
    E. 3

16. Jared can mow a lawn in 4 hours, while Rob can mow the same lawn in 6 hours. How long would it take to mow the lawn if Jared and Rob work together?

    A. 144 minutes

    B. 300 minutes

    C. 260 minutes

    D. 120 minutes

    E. 100 minutes

17. When riding his motorcycle, Chris travels 15 miles at 45 miles per hour, then an additional 20 miles at 35 miles per hour. What is the approximate average velocity of Chris' entire trip?

    A. 36 mph

    B. 39 mph

    C. 37 mph

    D. 38 mph

    E. 40 mph

9.10 Applied Mathematics – Solutions

1. **E.** Matt: m

   Nicole: m – 4

   Connor: 2(m – 4) – 2

2. **D.** Since the shape must be a square, all the side lengths must be equal. To find the area of a square, use the formula A = s^2. 16^2= 256, which is not enough since the area needs to be at least 275 square feet. 17^2 = 289, which is at least 275. Therefore, the answer is 17.

3. **D.** The DAT will have a couple of interest problems. The compound interest equation is A = $P(1+r)^n$, where A is the future value, P is the present value, r is the interest rate, and n is the number of years. In this case, P = 2.49, r = 0.03, and n = 4.

$$A= 2.49(1 + 0.03)^4 = 2.49(1.03)^4 = 2.49(1.1255...) = \$2.80$$

4. **D.** Using the distance formula, d = rt, calculate the time for each leg of the trip:

   25 = 50t; t = 1/2 hr.
   25 = 30t; t = 5/6 hr.

   Next, calculate the Average speed = Total distance/Total time

   $$\frac{50}{\left(\frac{1}{2}+\frac{5}{6}\right)} = \frac{50}{\frac{4}{3}} = 37\left(\frac{1}{2}\right) \text{ mph}$$

5. **E.** The album sells for $12.99 on iTunes, and there were 35,000 downloads. Therefore, the gross earnings are (12.99)(35,000) = $454,650. However, the boy band only gets 8% of this: (0.08)(454,650) = $36,372. They were given a $20,000 advance, so $36,372 - $20,000 = $16,372 left in royalties after the advance.

6. **C.** Because both gears' teeth are equally sized and shaped, we can use the teeth as units of circumference. The gears mesh without slipping, so the distance traveled along the circumference as the gears turn will be the same for both gears.

$$(10 \text{ teeth})(30 \text{ turns}) = (20 \text{ teeth})(x \text{ turns})$$

$$300 = 20x$$

$$x = 15 \text{ turns}$$

7. **D.** To answer the question, we can use the formula $A = P(1 - r)^t$, in which A is the current value at time t, t is the number of years of depreciation, P is the initial value, and r is the depreciation rate expressed as a decimal. Setting up and solving, we find that:

$$\$10{,}264 = P(1 - .25)^3$$

$$\$10{,}264 = P(.75)^3$$

$$\$10{,}264 = P(0.421875)^P = \$24{,}329$$

8. **B.** Adam orders 500 baseball cards, and 10% of them are unsellable, therefore he has $(.90)(500) = 450$ baseball cards that he can now sell.

   Adam paid $1000 for the cards and wants to make a 200% profit. This means he wants to earn $3000 total from the sales ($2000 in pure profit + $1000 to recover his costs).

   Set-up the following equation, where x is the price per card:

$$450x = 3000$$

$$x = \$6.67$$

9. **E.** To solve this problem, we can set-up the following expression to divide her total grade points (grade points multiplied by credits) earned by the total number of credits:

$$\frac{(4 \times 3) + (1 \times 4) + (3 \times 4) + (1 \times 2)}{4 + 1 + 3 + 1} = \frac{12 + 4 + 12 + 2}{4 + 1 + 3 + 1} = \frac{30}{9} = 3.33 \text{ GPA}$$

10. **E.** To answer this question, use the combined work formula:

$$\frac{1}{2} + \frac{1}{3} = \frac{1}{x}$$

x = 1.2 hrs. to paint one wall together

Now, calculate how much they will charge to paint a wall: (1.2)($50) = $60 to paint one wall. Therefore, 4 walls will cost (60)(4) = $240

11. **C.** To solve this problem, we can start by writing the following equation since the amount of iodine is constant after mixing:

$$(4*0.4) + (8*.12) = 12x$$

$$1.6 + 0.96 = 12x$$

$$2.56 = 12x$$

$$x = 0.213, \text{ or } 21.3\%$$

12. **C.** This problem can be easily solved by using a proportion:

$$\frac{100 \text{ miles}}{2 \text{ hours}} = \frac{x \text{ miles}}{9 \text{ hours}}$$

Cross-multiplying we get: 2x = 900; x = 450 miles

13. **E.** Andy can paint 1 wall in 6 hours, which means he paints ½ a wall in 3 hours. That means that ½ of the wall is still unpainted. If Brad takes 5 hours to paint a wall, it will take him 2.5 hours to paint the remaining ½ wall.

14. **C.** 5 boxes of cookies at $3 each = $15. But in this case, you will get 15 boxes for $15, which means each box really costs $1/box. $1(1.06) for the sale tax = $1.06/box.

15. **D.** To solve this problem, we should start by setting up an equation that represents the situation. We are told that Megan has 4 nickels, but we do not know how many quarters or dimes she has. Thus, we will represent the number of quarters with the variable x, and the number of dimes as (11 – x), because the number of dimes will be (15 total coins – 4 nickels – x quarters).

$$(0.05 \text{ x } 4) + 0.25x + 0.10(11 – x) = 2.20$$

$$0.20 + 0.25x + 1.10 – 0.10x = 2.20$$

$$.15x + 1.30 = 2.20$$

$$.15x = 0.90$$

$$x = 6$$

Therefore, Megan has 6 quarters, 4 nickels, and 5 dimes.

16. **A.** To solve this problem, use the combined work formula.

Note that all the answer choices are in minutes, so convert hours to minutes:

$$\frac{1}{240 \text{ minutes}} + \frac{1}{360 \text{ minutes}} = \frac{1}{x}$$

$$x = 144 \text{ minutes}$$

17. **B.** To calculate his average velocity, we need to calculate the total time Chris spent traveling, and then divide the total distance by the total time traveled.

To calculate the total time, divide the distance by speed:

$$\frac{15 \text{ miles}}{45 \text{ miles per hour}} = \frac{1}{3} \text{hrs}$$

$$\frac{20 \text{ miles}}{35 \text{ miles per hour}} = \frac{4}{7} \text{hrs}$$

Therefore, Chris has been riding his motorcycle for a total of $1/3 + 4/7 = 19/21$ hours.

Now, we can divide the total distance by the total time to find average speed:

$$\frac{15 \text{ miles} + 20 \text{ miles}}{\frac{19}{21} \text{ hours}} = 35 \text{ miles x } (21/19) = 39 \text{ mph}$$

Chapter 10: Probabilities and Statistics

10.1 Vocabulary

- **Median**: the **middle number** in a group of numbers arranged in numerical order. To find the median, set all the numbers in **increasing order**, and the middle number is the median. In an **odd number of digits,** the median is the **middle number**, and in an **even number of digits**, the median is **the average of the two middle numbers**

- **Mode**: the **most frequent number** in a set of numbers. Note that a set can have more than one mode if these numbers have the same frequency, or can have no mode if each number only appears once

- **Average**: the arithmetic mean, or **the sum of the numbers divided by the number of digits being averaged** (i.e., the average of 3, 5, 6 and 10 = 24/4 = 6)

- **Range**: the **difference between the lowest and highest value** (largest number – smallest number). i.e., the range of 1, 3, 4, 6, 11, 23 is 22 (23-1)

- **Standard Deviation**: measures **the average distance between the values in a data set and the mean**

- A **small standard deviation** means that the **data values tend to be very close to the mean**; a **large standard deviation** means that the **data values spread out over an extensive range of values**

- To **calculate standard deviation**, first, compute the difference of each data value from the mean, and then square each result. Next, add the average of these values, and take the square root

- The standard deviation has the same units of measure as the original data

$$\text{Standard deviation: } \sqrt{\sum \frac{(x_i - \mu)^2}{n}}$$

$$\text{Mean: } \sum \frac{x_i}{n}$$

$$\text{Variance: } \sum \frac{(x_i - \mu)^2}{n}$$

DAT TIP: When you are given multiple data sets and are asked which data set has the largest standard deviation, **find the range** (largest value minus the smallest value). **This will determine which data is most spread, and thus should have the largest standard deviation.**

10.2 The Empirical Rule

- Around **68%** of the data is within **1 standard deviation** above and below the mean
- Around **95%** of the data is within **2 standard deviations** above and below the mean
- Around **99.7%** of the data is within **3 standard deviations** above and below the mean

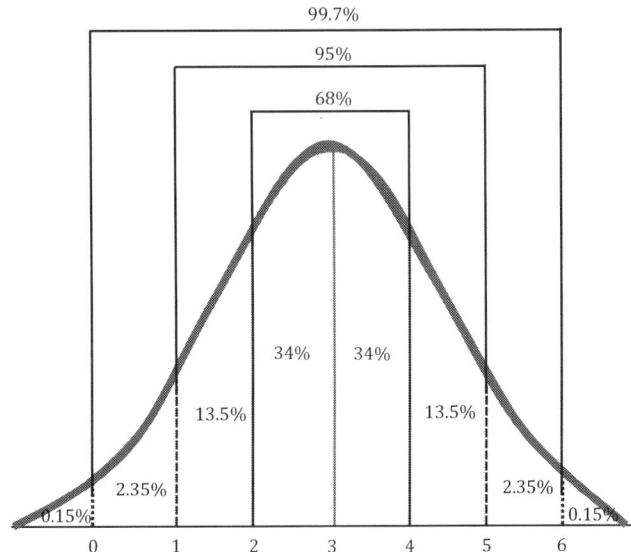

Example: **The population of lions in the Miami zoo is normally distributed. If, on average, each lion lives 13.1 years, and the standard deviation of the lions lifespan is 1.5 years, what is the probability that a lion in the Miami zoo will live longer than 14.6 years?**

Knowing that the mean is 13.1, the following age ranges fall within each standard deviation:
- One standard deviation ($\mu \pm \sigma$): (13.1 - 1.5) to (13.1 + 1.5), or 11.6 to 14.6
- Two standard deviations ($\mu \pm 2\sigma$): 13.1 - (2 x 1.5) to 13.1 + (2 x 1.5), or 10.1 to 16.1
- Three standard deviations ($\mu \pm 3\sigma$): 13.1 - (3 x 1.5) to 13.1 + (3 x 1.5), or, 8.6 to 17.6

The question asks for the probability of a lion living 14.6 years or longer. The empirical rule shows that 68% of the distribution lies within one standard deviation, in this case, from 11.6 to 14.6 years. Thus, the remaining 32% of the distribution lies outside this range. One half lies above 14.6 and the other below 11.6. So, the probability of a lion living for more than 14.6 is 16% (calculated as 32% divided by two).

10.3 Combination and Permutation

- **Permutation:** the arrangement of **r items selected out of n items**. Permutation is used for questions asking, **"how many ways/ arrangements / orders are possible?"**

- **Combination:** the selection of **r items taken out of n items, where the order does not matter.** Combination is used for questions asking, **"how many subgroups can be chosen from a larger group?"**

DAT Tip: Follow the proceeding table to determine which formula to use in combination and permutation problems.

iPrepDental – 2025 Quantitative Reasoning Notes

Repetition Allowed?	Order matters	Use	Formula	Example Question	Example solution
Yes	Yes	Permutation	n^r	In how many ways can you form a password consisted of 4 digits?	Since the numbers can be repeated, and we have 10 options (0-9): $10^4 = 10,000$
No	Yes	Permutation	$\dfrac{n!}{(n-r)!}$	In how many ways can a president, a treasurer and a secretary be chosen from a group of 5 candidates?	**Reasoning:** the 1st position has 5 possible choices, the 2nd 4, and the 3rd 3, thus: 5x4x3= 60 **Formula:** $\dfrac{5!}{(5-3)!} = \dfrac{120}{2} = 60$
No	No	Combination	$\dfrac{n!}{r!\,(n-r)!}$	How many different committees of 3 people can be chosen from 5 people?	In choosing a committee, order doesn't matter; so, we need the number of combinations of 3 people out of 5: $\dfrac{5!}{3!\,2!} = \dfrac{120}{12} = 1$

To calculate the number of n objects where there are $n_1, n_2 \ldots n_k$ repeated items, use the formula:

$$\frac{n!}{n_1!\; n_2! \ldots \ldots n_k!}$$

Example: In how many ways the word Mississippi can be arranged?

The word Mississippi is composed of 11 letters. We have one m, four i, four s, and two p:

$$\frac{11!}{1!\,4!\,4!\,2!} = \frac{11 \times 10 \times 9 \times 8 \times 7 \times 6 \times 5 \times 4 \times 3 \times 2 \times 1}{(1)(4 \times 3 \times 2 \times 1)(4 \times 3 \times 2 \times 1)(2 \times 1)} = 34,650$$

10.4 Finding the Number of Permutations of n Distinct Objects

The **Multiplication Principle** states that if one event can occur in m ways and a second event can occur in n ways after the first event has occurred, the **two events can occur in m×n ways**.

Examples:

Denny's has a breakfast special that includes a sandwich, a side dish, and a beverage. There are three types of sandwiches, four side dishes, and five beverage choices. What is the total number of possible breakfast specials?

Using the multiplication rule: 3 x 4 x 5 = 60

At a swimming competition, six swimmers compete in a race. How many ways can they be placed in the first, second, and third positions?

Using the multiplication rule: 6 x 5 x 4 = 120

Note that the first place has 6 options, the second place has 5, and the third has 4.

10.5 Probability

Probability describes the **chances or likelihood of an event/s to take place**. It is expressed as the ratio (fraction) of the desired outcome/s to the total number of possible outcome/s.

$$\text{Probability} = \frac{\text{Number of possible outcomes}}{\text{Number of desired outcome}}$$

The probability of any event cannot exceed 1 or be less than zero. Note that **1 means 100% chance of an event occurring, and 0 means no chances (0%) of an event happening.**

The sum of the probabilities of all outcomes of a specific event must equal 1. Note that **the probability that an event does not occur is one minus the probability that the event does occur**. For example, if the probability of rain tomorrow is 1/3, then the probability that it will not rain tomorrow is (1-1/3) = 2/3.

DAT STUDY TIP: AND = multiply, OR = add

Example: **What is the probability of picking a red ball twice from a bag containing six blue balls, and three red balls, without replacement?**

The probability of picking any color ball from a bag is the number of balls of that color divided by the total number of balls. There are three red balls, and a total of nine balls in the bag; therefore, the probability of picking a red ball is 3/9 or 1/3. If that ball is removed, we have a total of 8 balls and only 2 red balls. Therefore, the probability of picking a 2nd red ball is 2/8 or 1/4.
The probability that both these events happen (the 1st is red AND the 2nd is red, without replacement) is: 1/4 x 1/3= 1/12.

Note that if the question stated with replacement, the probability would have been 1/3 x 1/3.
Also note that if the question asked for one color OR the other, you would have needed to ADD the two probabilities.

10.6 Coin Flipping Problems

A coin is fair. That means that **each flip has an equal chance of being a head or a tail**; thus, the probability **of getting a head or a tail is ½.** Each toss is an independent event since the outcome is independent of the previous result.

Examples:

If a coin is flipped three times, what is the probability of getting a tail each time?

When you flip a coin, the chance of getting a tail is 1/2. This is true every time you flip the coin; therefore, if you flip it three times, the chances of you getting a tail each time is 1/2 x 1/2 x 1/2, or 1/8.

If you flip a coin twice, what is the probability of getting one head and one tail?

The question didn't specify a particular order, and therefore, we must account for two scenarios: (Getting a head and then a tail) OR (Getting a tail and then a head) = (H, T) or (T, H) = (1/2 x 1/2) + (1/2 x 1/2) = 1/4 + 1/4 = 2/4 = 1/2 = 0.5

Note that we added the two probabilities due to the word OR.

10.7 Deck of Cards Problems

A standard deck of cards has 52 cards. The **probability** of drawing any **random card from a deck of cards is 1/52.** Each card can be categorized into **four suits, constituting 13 cards each** (1 Ace, 3 face cards, and 9 number cards). The suits that are represented by red cards are hearts and diamonds, while the suits that are represented by black cards are spades and clubs. There are 26 red cards and 26 black cards. Face cards (Kings, Queens, and Jacks) in all four suits.

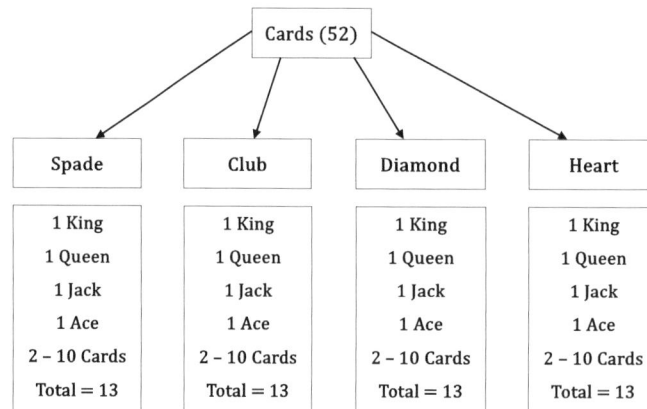

		Cards (52)	
Spade	**Club**	**Diamond**	**Heart**
1 King	1 King	1 King	1 King
1 Queen	1 Queen	1 Queen	1 Queen
1 Jack	1 Jack	1 Jack	1 Jack
1 Ace	1 Ace	1 Ace	1 Ace
2 – 10 Cards	2 – 10 Cards	2 – 10 Cards	2 – 10 Cards
Total = 13	Total = 13	Total = 13	Total = 13

Example 1: What is the probability of drawing a King from a deck of cards?

There are 52 cards in a deck of cards. Hence, the total number of outcomes = 52. The number of favorable outcomes = 4 (as there are 4 Kings in a deck). Therefore, the probability of this event occurring is 4/52 = 1/13

Example 2: Rana has drawn a card from a well-shuffled deck. Help her find the probability of the card being red or a King.

The total number of outcomes = 52. There are 26 red cards and 4 cards that are Kings. However, 2 of the red cards are Kings. If we add 26 and 4, we will count these two cards twice. Thus, the correct number of favorable outcomes is 26 + 4 - 2 = 28. Hence, the probability of an event occurring is 28/52 = 7/13

10.8 Dice Problems

Recall that probabilities are calculated using the simple formula: Probability = number of desired outcomes ÷ number of possible outcomes. Therefore, **the probability of getting any of the six numbers when rolling a six-sided die is** $\frac{1}{6}$ **= 0.167, or 16.7 percent chance.**

Examples:

What is the probability of rolling a 2 and 6 when rolling two dice?

Getting a 2 and a 6 are two independent probabilities. When we need the probability of one event **AND** the probability of another independent event, we **MULTIPLY** the two probabilities:

$1/6 \times 1/6 = 1/36 = 1 \div 36 = 0.0278$, or 2.78 percent.

What is the probability of getting a sum of less than five OR at least ten, with a pair of standard six-sided dice?

For two dice, the total number of ways to roll the dice is 36 (6 on the first die can go with any of the six on the second die)

The following outcomes result in a **sum of less than 5**: {1, 1} {1, 2} {1, 3} {2, 1} {2, 2} {3, 1}, for **6 possible outcomes.**

The following outcomes result in a **sum of at least 10**: {4, 6} {5, 6} {5, 5} {6, 6} {6, 5} {6, 4} for **6 possible outcomes.**

Since we are looking for a sum of less than five **OR** a sum of at least ten, we **ADD** the total number of desired outcomes. Therefore, the probability of getting less than five, or at least ten is 6/36 + 6/ 36 = 12/36, or 1/3

If two six-sided dice are rolled, then what is the probability that the sum of the two dice is seven?

The easiest way to solve this problem is to consult the table below. You will notice that are six possible outcomes where the sum of the two dice is equal to seven. The number of total possible outcomes remains 36. We find the probability by dividing the event frequency (6) by the size of the sample space (36), resulting in a probability of 1/6.

DAT TIP: Memorize the table below for faster calculations on the DAT

Sum of Two Dice	Number of Ways
2	1
3	2
4	3
5	4
6	5
7	6
8	5
9	4
10	3
11	2
12	1
Total	**36**

10.9 Venn Diagram

Venn diagrams are used in word problems asking for the union/ intersection of two or more sets. The shaded area is the intersection of the two sets (elements that are common to both sets). The union includes the elements of either set.

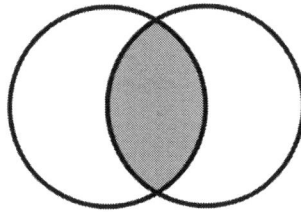

Examples:

Among 83 students, 51 take AP chemistry, and 25 take AP statistics. Of the students taking AP chemistry and statistics, 11 take both classes. How many students are not taking either class?

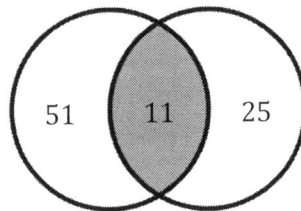

If 11 students are taking both classes, 40 (51-11) are only taking AP chemistry, and 14 (25-11) are only taking AP statistics. The number of people taking at least one course, therefore, is 40 + 14 + 11 = 65. The 83 members minus the 65 that are taking courses leave 18 who are not taking any courses.

Old McDonald's has a farm. Some of his cows are used for milk, some for reproduction, and some for both. If among old McDonalds 40 cows, ten are only used for milk, and three are used for both milk and reproduction, how many cows are used for reproduction?

Since we know that only 10 cows are used for milk, we must subtract this number from the total number of cows to get our answer: 40 – 10 = 30 cows. The cows that do both are still used for reproduction, so the correct answer is 30 cows.

Among 100 Biology students, 70 students joined the pre - dental club, 40 joined the pre-med club, and 10 joined neither. How many students joined the pre-dental and the pre-med clubs?

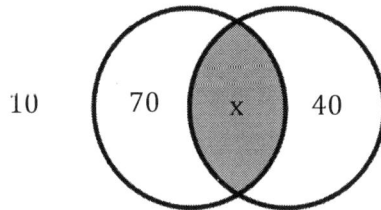

10   70   x   40

To solve this question, draw a Venn diagram and find the intersection. We have one circle of 70 and another with 40. We should get 100 students when we add the two circles plus the ten students who joined neither. However, when adding the two circles, we add the intersections twice; therefore, we need to subtract the intersection once. We get $70+40-\text{intersection}+10=100$, which means the intersection is 20.

10.10 Probabilities and Statistics – Practice Problems

1. Left-handed people make up 1 out of every 10 people. If you lined up all the students in a school, what is the probability of having the first 30 people not being left-handed?

    A. $(0.9)^{30}$

    B. 0.1×0.9^{30}

    C. $(0.1)^{30}$

    D. 30×0.9

    E. $30 \times 0.9 \times 0.1$

2. If a six-sided fair die is rolled 3 times in a row, what is the probability that a "5" is rolled the first time, but not the second or third time?

    A. 25/216

    B. 25/36

    C. 25/18

    D. 1/125

    E. 8/27

3. A bag contains 5 blue, 3 yellow, and 4 red marbles. 4 marbles are randomly drawn without replacement from the bag. What is the probability that none of the 4 marbles drawn is yellow?

    A. 9/8

    B. 3/8

    C. 3/4

    D. 81/256

    E. 14/55

4. A student will participate in two math competitions: an algebra competition, and a geometry competition. The probability of the student coming in first place in the algebra competition is 25%, and the probability of the student coming in first place in the geometry competition is 20%. If the student completes in both competitions, what is the probability he comes in first place in exactly one of the competitions?

   A. 1/5

   B. 3/20

   C. 4/25

   D. 7/20

   E. 4/20

5. 30 tennis players compete in a tournament. Each player will play a game with every other player exactly once during the tournament. How many games are played during the tournament?

   A. 435

   B. 50

   C. 60

   D. 525

   E. 400

6. Lisa picks two letters at random from the word STATISTICS, with replacement. What is the probability that she picks both times a vowel?

   A. 1/15

   B. 3/50

   C. 3/10

   D. 9/100

   E. 9/10

7. Which of the following data sets has the largest standard deviation?

    A. {1, 2, 3, 4, 5}

    B. {2, 4, 6, 8, 10}

    C. {2, 3, 5, 7, 8}

    D. {1, 2, 3, 5, 7}

    E. {2, 3, 4, 5, 6}

8. There are 10 marbles in a bag: 5 red, 3 blue, and 2 green. What is the probability of two randomly chosen marbles without replacement, that 1 is red, and 1 is green?

    A. 2/9

    B. 1/9

    C. 1/3

    D. 1/10

    E. 7/10

9. The even numbers on a regular die are painted red. On a second regular die, the prime numbers are painted blue. If both dice are thrown, then what is the probability that both come up red?

    A. 1/12

    B. 3/4

    C. 1/2

    D. 1/3

    E. ¼

10. How many ways (orders) can you arrange 5 different playing cards?

    A. 120

    B. 720

    C. 5

    D. 25

    E. 125

11. How many ways can you choose 6 people from a group of 12?

    A. 72

    B. 847

    C. 1022

    D. 924

    E. 679

12. Doug has 7 dress shirts and 5 pairs of pants. How many different combinations of one dress shirt and one pair of pants can he make?

    A. 7

    B. 14

    C. 35

    D. 25

    E. 12

13. How many distinct ways can 2 people sit in a 7- seat minivan?

 A. 42

 B. 14

 C. 9

 D. 50

 E. 36

10.11 Probabilities and Statistics – Solutions

1. **A.** If 1 out of 10 people is left-handed, that means each person has a 0.1 chance of being left-handed. Each person has a 1 – 0.1 or 0.9 chance of not being left-handed (being right-handed). We need to find the probability of all these independent events, which means we must multiply the possibilities of 30 people, or simply 0.9^{30}

2. **A.** Each time the fair die is rolled, there is a 1/6 chance of "five" being the top face. Therefore, the chance of "five" not being the top face is 5/6 (1 – 1/6 = 5/6). To find the probability of the outcome the problem describes, we need to multiply the probability of getting a 5, which is (1/6) times the probability of not getting a 5, which is (5/6), twice:

$$(1/6)(5/6)(5/6) = 25/216$$

3. **E.** Because the marbles are drawn without replacement, each draw will diminish the total amount of marbles left to draw from. The question is asking for the probability of not getting yellow, which is equal to the probability of getting a blue or red marbles four times. In the first draw, we have 9 red and blue marbles, in the second, we are left with 8, in the third draw we have 7, and in the fourth we have 6:

$$P(\text{none yellow}) = (9/12)(8/11)(7/10)(6/9) = 3024/11880 = 14/55$$

4. **D.** The question does not specify which competition is won, so we must consider two different scenarios: the student comes in first place in the algebra competition but does not come in first in the geometry competition, or the student does not come in first in the algebra competition but comes in first in the geometry competition:

P(1st in algebra, not 1st geometry): (25%)(80%) = (1/4)(4/5) = 1/5

P(not 1st algebra, 1st in geometry): (75%)(20%) = (3/4)(1/5) = 3/20

The total probability that the student comes in first place in exactly one competitionis found by adding the probabilities of the two distinct scenarios:

$$1/5 + 3/20 = 4/20 + 3/20 = 7/20$$

5. **A.** For each game played, we must select 2 players from a group of 30 players. The order of the 2 players does not matter (for example, it does not matter if Jen plays Mark, or if Mark plays Jen). Therefore, we use the combination formula when the order does NOT matter:

C(n,r) = [n!/r!(n-r)!] where n is the number of games and r is the 2 players chosen at a time:

$$\frac{30!}{2!\,(30-2)!} = \frac{30!}{2!\,(28!)}$$

Recall that a "!" sign in math means factorial, which is a product of every consecutive whole number from 1 to the given number. Therefore, 30! is 30 x 29 x 28 x 27.... all the way down to 1, etc. Note that the factors in 28! cancel with those same factors found within 30! Resulting in:

$$\frac{30 \times 29}{2 \times 1} = \frac{870}{2} = 435$$

6. **D.** There are 3 vowels (A, I, I) in the word STATISTICS, and 10 letters total. Therefore, the probability of choosing a vowel on the first letter is 3/10. Because the letter she chooses is put back, the chance of getting a vowel on the second try is also 3/10. Therefore, using the multiplication rule, the probability of both events occurring is: $(3/10)(3/10) = 9/100$

7. **B.** For this kind of problem, do NOT attempt to find the standard deviation of every answer choice until you find the largest one. Since standard deviation is a measure of spread in a data set and variation in the values, a data set with a large standard deviation will have a larger spread of values and usually a larger range. To calculate the range, subtract the highest number minus the lowest number in the data set. In the case of choice [B], this is 10 - 2 = 8

8. **A.** problem does not specify a specific order in which the red and green marbles must be drawn from the bag. To solve this problem, you must calculate the probability of getting a red marble first, then a green one, OR a green marble first, then a red one. The probability of getting red then green: $(5/10)(2/9) = 1/9$ Probability of getting green then red: $(2/10)(5/9) = 1/9$. Using the addition rule, the probability of either event occurring would be $1/9 + 1/9 = 2/9$

9. **E.** On the first die, only the even numbers are painted. Therefore, 2, 4, and 6 are painted, and thus, the probability of rolling a red number is 3/6, or ½. On the second die, only the prime numbers are painted blue. The definition of a prime number is any whole number (not including 0 and 1) whose only factors are 1 and itself. 2, 3, and 5 are the prime numbers on a regular die, making the probability of the second die 3/6, or ½. Using the multiplication rule, $(1/2)(1/2) = 1/4$

10. **A.** There are five positions for the first card, four remaining positions for the second card, three remaining positions for the third card, etc. Therefore, the answer to this problem is 5 x 4 x 3 x 2 x 1 = 120, or in other words, 5!

11. **D.** Since we are not told that order matters, use the combination formula:

C(n,r) = [n!/r!(n-r)!]

$$\frac{12!}{6!\,(12-6)!}$$

The easiest thing to do is cross cancel factors to make the multiplying easier. 12! =12 x 11 x 10 x 9…etc. and 6! = 6 x 5 x 4…. So, the factors in the first 6! will cancel with those same factors in 12! leaving you with:

$$\frac{12 \times 11 \times 10 \times 9 \times 8 \times 7}{6 \times 5 \times 4 \times 3 \times 2 \times 1} = \frac{665280}{720} = 924$$

12. **C.** There are seven shirt possibilities and five pants possibilities; thus, the total number of options is $7(5) = 35$ (using the multiplication rule)

13. **A.** In this problem, order does matter since if 2 people switch seats, that is a new way for them to be sitting. Therefore, the permutation formula can be used: $_nP_r = \frac{n!}{(n-r)!}$

"n" represents the sample size, in this case 7. "r" represents the number of selections, in this case 2.

$$_7P_2 = \frac{7!}{(7-2)!} = \frac{7!}{5!} = \frac{7 \times 6 \times 5 \times 4 \times 3 \times 2 \times 1}{5 \times 4 \times 3 \times 2 \times 1} = 7 \times 6 = 42$$

Chapter 11: Geometry

Although Geometry is no longer officially on the DAT, the ADA recently indicated that the **quantitative comparison section is not limited to geometry questions**. To avoid any "surprises" on the DAT, we urge you to learn the following concepts and formulas:

11.1 Special Right Triangles

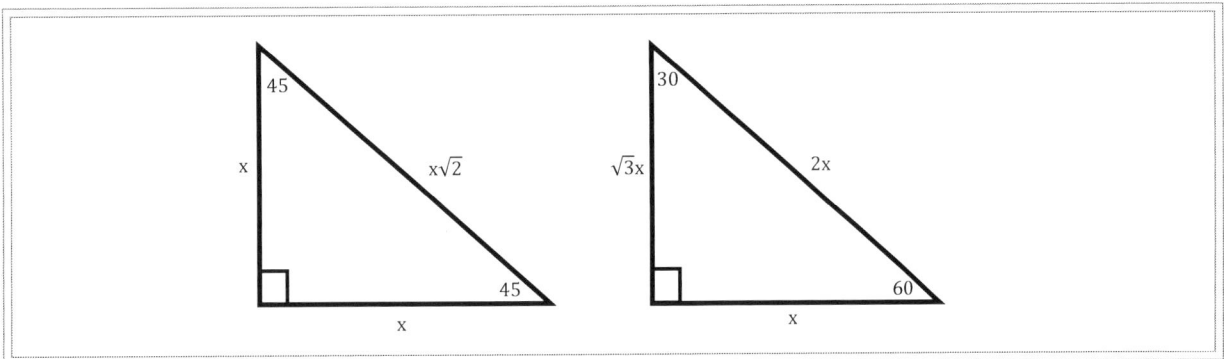

11.2 Pythagorean Theorem

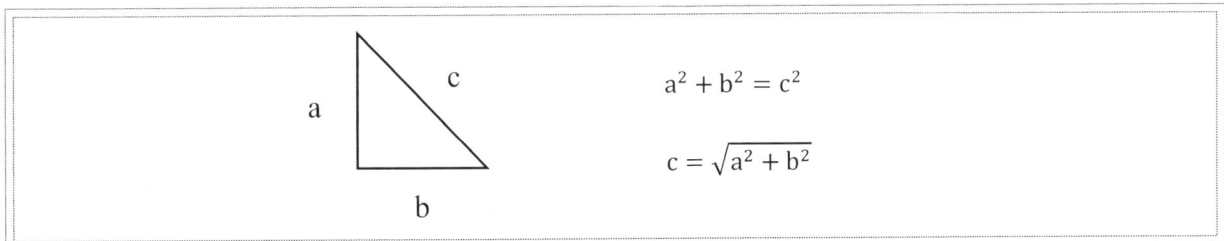

$$a^2 + b^2 = c^2$$

$$c = \sqrt{a^2 + b^2}$$

Pythagorean Triplets

Pythagorean triples consists of three positive integers a, b, and c such that $a^2 + b^2 = c^2$. When a triangle side are Pythagorean, it's a right triangle.

- 3, 4, 5
- 5, 12, 13
- 7, 24, 25
- 8, 15, 17

DAT TIP: any side of a triangle is always smaller than the sum of the two other sides.

11.3 The Ellipse Equation

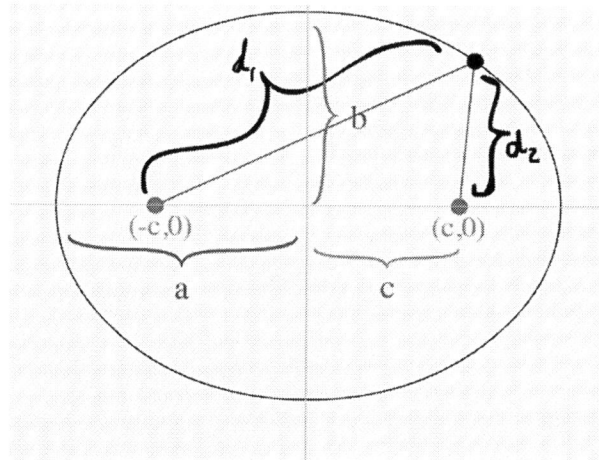

a: Major axis
b: Minor axis
c: Focus point

$$b^2 = a^2 - c^2$$

$$\frac{x^2}{a^2} + \frac{y^2}{b^2} = 1$$

11.4 The Circle Equation

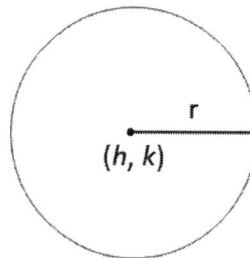

$$(x-h)^2 + (y-k)^2 = r^2$$

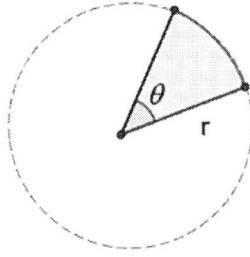

If θ is measured in degrees, then **Area of Sector** $= \dfrac{\theta}{360°} \times \pi r^2$

If θ is measured in radians, then **Area of Sector** $= \dfrac{1}{2} r^2 \theta$

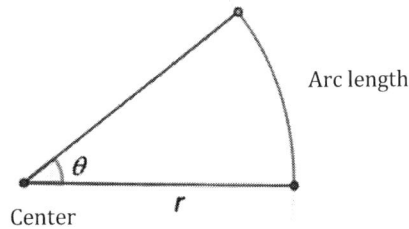

If θ is measured in degrees, then **Arc Length** $= \dfrac{\theta}{360°} \times 2\pi r$

If θ is measured in radians, then **Arc Length** $= \theta r$

Impact of Increasing the Radius of a Circle

- The **circle's circumference** will **increase by the same factor the radius increase**. For example, if you double the radius, the circumference will double.

- The **area of a circle** will **exponentially increase when the radius increase**. For example, if you double the radius, the area will increase by a factor of 4

11.5 Formulas

Square

- Area $= s^2$
- Perimeter $= 4s$

Rectangle

- Area $= lw$
- Perimeter $= 2l + 2w$

Circle

- Area $= \pi r^2$
- Perimeter $= 2\pi r$

Ellipse

- Surface area $= \pi ab$

Triangle

- Area $= \frac{1}{2}bh$
- Perimeter $= a + b + c$

Parallelogram

- Area $= bh$
- Perimeter $= 2a + 2b$

Wheel

- Area $= \pi(R^2 - r^2)$

Cube

- Area $= 6l^2$
- Volume $= l^3$

Circular Sector

- Area $= \pi r^2 \frac{\theta}{360°}$
- Length $= \pi r \frac{\theta}{180°}$

Trapezoid

- Area $= h\frac{a+b}{2}$
- Perimeter $= a + b + c + d$

Rectangular Prism

- Area $= 2ab + 2ac + 2bc$
- Volume $= abc$

Pyramid

- Volume $= \frac{lwh}{3}$

Cylinder

- Area $= 2\pi r(r + h)$
- Volume $= \pi r^2 h$

Cone

- Area $= \pi r^2 + \pi rs$
- Surface area $= \sqrt{r^2 + h^2}$
- Volume $= \frac{1}{3}\pi r^2 h$

Sphere

- Surface area $= 4\pi r^2$
- Volume $= \frac{4}{3}\pi r^3$

Frustum of Cone

- Volume $= \frac{1}{3}\pi h(r^2 + rR + R^2)$

Regular Polygons

- Sum of exterior angles $= 360$
- **Measure of an exterior angle $= \frac{360}{n}$**
- Sum of interior angles $= (n - 2)180$
- **Measure of an interior angle $= \frac{(n-2)180}{n}$**
- Number of diagonal lines $= \frac{n(n-3)}{2}$

11.6 Geometry – Practice Problems

1. If the area of square DEFG is equal to the area of triangle ABC, then how long is line AC?

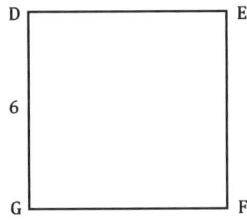

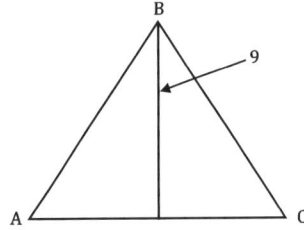

    A. 4

    B. 6

    C. 8

    D. 9

    E. 10

2. A cube has side lengths of 8 inches. If the cube is divided into blocks with dimensions of 1x2x2 inches, what is the maximum number of blocks that can form?

    A. 16

    B. 32

    C. 128

    D. 256

    E. 156

3. A triangle has side lengths of 5, 12, and 13. A second triangle has side lengths of 8, 15, and 17. What is the ratio of the area of the smaller triangle to the area of the larger triangle?

   A. 1/2

   B. 7/10

   C. 2/3

   D. 4/5

   E. 5/6

4. Circle A and circle B are respectively defined in the standard coordinate plane by the equations $(x + 2)^2 + (y - 4)^2 = 16$ and $(x - 3)^2 + (y + 5)^2 = 25$. What is the shortest distance between the center of circle A and the center of circle B?

   A. $2\sqrt{14}$

   B. $5\sqrt{3}$

   C. $\sqrt{106}$

   D. 10

   E. $2\sqrt{7}$

5. A water pitcher has an interior space in the shape of a cylinder with a diameter of 6 inches and a height of 10 inches. Each set of cups has an interior space in the shape of a cylinder with a diameter of 2 inches and a height of 5 inches. If the pitcher is filled with water, how many cups can then be filled to the brim from the pitcher without refilling the pitcher?

   A. 17

   B. 18

   C. 16

   D. 15

   E. 14

6. What is the diameter of a sphere that has a volume equal to 6 times its surface area?

   A. 12

   B. 48

   C. 24

   D. 18

   E. 36

7. Two lines in the coordinate plane are perpendicular. If one line passes through the points (-3, 2) and (5, 7), what is the slope of the other line?

   A. 5/8

   B. -8/5

   C. 2/5

   D. 5/2

   E. -5/2

8. A square of side length 2 has two half-circles etched into it as shown in the figure below. What area of the square is outside of either of the half-circles?

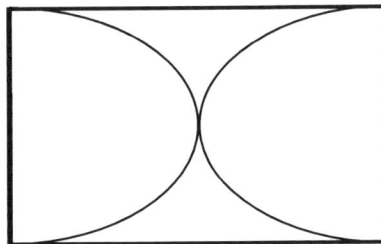

   A. π/2 – 4

   B. π – 4

   C. 4 – π/2

   D. 4 – π

   E. 1 – π/4

9. The hypotenuse of a right triangle has a length of 15, and one of its sides has a length of 9. What is the area of the triangle?

    A. 67.5

    B. 135

    C. 108

    D. 54

    E. 90

11.7 Geometry – Solutions

1. **C.** The area of a square is S², thus, the area of DEFG is $6^2 = 36$

   The area of triangle ABC can be found by using the formula A = 1/2bh

   $$36 = ½(x)(9)$$

   $$72 = 9x$$

   $$x = 8$$

2. **C.** A cube's volume is the side length cubed (s³). Thus, the cube has a volume of 8 x 8 x 8, or 512 units. Each block has a volume of 1 x 2 x 2, or a total volume of 4 units. Thus, the number of blocks that can be formed = 512/4 or 128.

3. **A.** It should be immediately noticed that the given triangle side lengths are Pythagorean Triples, which means the 2 smaller lengths from each set would have to be the legs (used for the base and the height to find the area).

   Triangle 5, 12, 13: A = ½(5)(12) = 30

   Triangle 8, 15, 17: A = ½(8)(15) = 60

   30/60 = ½

4. **C.** The equation of a circle is $(x - h)^2 + (y - k)^2 = r^2$, where (h,k) is the center. Therefore, Circle A's center is at (-2, 4) and Circle B's center is at (3, -5). The shortest distance between two points can be found by using the distance formula:

   $$\text{Distance} = \sqrt{(x_2 - x_1)^2 + (y_2 - y_1)^2}$$

   $$\text{Distance} = \sqrt{(-2 - 3)^2 + (4 - (-5))^2}$$

   $$\text{Distance} = \sqrt{(-5)^2 + (9)^2}$$

   $$\text{Distance} = \sqrt{25 + 81}$$

   $$\text{Distance} = \sqrt{106}$$

5. **B.** The volume of a cylinder is given by the area of the cylinder's base multiplied by the cylinder's height, represented as $V_{cylinder} = \pi(r)^2 \times h$. We can use this formula to calculate the volume of the pitcher and the volume of a cup, and then divide to determine how many cups can be filled from the pitcher:

Volume of pitcher $= \pi \times (3)^2(10) = 90\pi$

Volume of cup $= \pi \times (1)^2(5) = 5\pi$

$$\frac{\text{Volume of pitcher}}{\text{Volume of cup}} = \frac{90\pi}{5\pi} = 18 \text{ cups}$$

6. **E.**

$$\text{Volume}_{sphere} = \frac{4}{3}\pi r^3$$

$$\text{Surface Area}_{sphere} = 4\pi r^2$$

We can use the formulas to set-up an equation, solve for the radius, and then double the radius to get the diameter:

$$\frac{4}{3}\pi r^3 = 6(4\pi r^2)$$

$$\frac{4}{3}\pi r^3 = 24\pi r^2$$

$$\pi r^3 = 18\pi r^2$$

$$r^3 = 18r^2$$

$$\frac{r^3}{r^2} = 18$$

$$r = 18, \text{ which makes } d = 18(2) = 36$$

7. **B.** Perpendicular lines have negative (opposite), reciprocal slopes. Find the slope of the given line, and then take the reciprocal to get the slope of a line perpendicular to it:

$$\text{slope} = \frac{y_2 - y_1}{x_2 - x_1}$$

$$\text{slope} = \frac{7 - 2}{5 - (-3)} = \frac{5}{8}$$

If the slope of the given line is 5/8, then the slope of a line perpendicular to it is -8/5.

8. **D.** To solve this problem, we should first find the area occupied by the half circles. The two half circles can be combined to form a circle with a diameter of 2, thus we can find the area of a circle with a radius of 1:

$$A = \pi r^2$$

$$A = \pi(1)^2$$

$$A = \pi$$

Next, find the area of the square:

$$A = s^2$$

$$A = (2)^2$$

$$A = 4$$

Note that the asked area is the difference between the square and the two half circles; therefore, the area outside each of the half circles is 4 – π

9. **D.** If you recognize that the given sides are from the special right triangle 3-4-5, then the remaining side must be side length 12 (triangle 9-12-15). If not, you could also use the Pythagorean Theorem to find the missing side, since you are given the lengths of one leg and the hypotenuse. We can use 9 and 12 as the base and height, respectively, to find the area of the triangle:

$$A = 1/2(b)(h)$$

$$A = 1/2(9)(12) = 54$$

Made in the USA
Columbia, SC
27 May 2025